LIT
ENC
OF

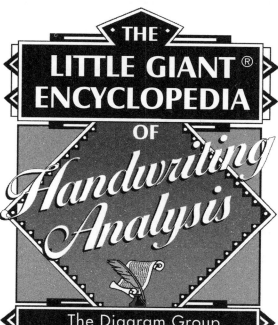

THE LITTLE GIANT® ENCYCLOPEDIA

OF

Handwriting Analysis

The Diagram Group

Sterling Publishing Co., Inc.
New York

Library of Congress Cataloging-in-Publication Data

The little giant encyclopedia of handwriting analysis / the
    Diagram Group.
        p.   cm.
    Includes index.
    ISBN 0-8069-1831-4
    1. Graphology. I. Diagram Group.
    BF891.L58   1999
    155.2'82—DC21   99–39410
                                                     CIP

10 9 8 7 6 5 4 3 2 1

Published by Sterling Publishing Company, Inc.
387 Park Avenue South, New York, N.Y. 10016
A Diagram Book first created by Diagram Information Visual
Limited of Kentish Town Road, London NW5 2JU
© 1999 by Diagram Information Visual Limited
Distributed in Canada by Sterling Publishing
c/o Canadian Manda Group, One Atlantic Avenue, Suite 105
Toronto, Ontario, Canada M6K 3E7
Distributed in Great Britain and Europe by Cassell PLC
Wellington House, 125 Strand, London WC2R 0BB, England
Distributed in Australia by Capricorn Link (Australia) Pty Ltd.
P.O. Box 6651, Baulkham Hills, Business Centre, NSW 2153,
Australia
Manufactured in the United States of America

Sterling ISBN 0-8069-1831-4

FOREWORD

The *Little Giant Encyclopedia of Handwriting Analysis* is a fully illustrated, comprehensive guide to the kinds of character traits that can be revealed by handwriting. Working through each section of the book the reader is shown how to analyze a sample of handwriting in order to answer a whole range of questions concerning the likely character traits of the writer, including:

- What can you tell about a person by the way he or she addresses an envelope?
- What does it mean if someone uses red ink?
- What kind of people use colored paper?
- How can you tell whether someone is feeling positive about the future?
- What does it mean when someone writes in the margin?
- What do wide spaces between words reveal?
- How can you tell whether someone writes fast or slow and what does it mean?
- What kind of mood are you in when you use heavy pressure when writing?
- Does it matter if your handwriting slants to the left?
- How can you tell if someone is likely to be aggressive, ambitious, artistic, cultured, defensive, diplomatic, dishonest, dreamy, egotistic, enterprising, fussy, generous, greedy, gregarious, honest, imaginative, independent, intelligent, loyal, materialistic, neurotic, opinionated, protective, quarrelsome, resentful, reserved, secretive, talkative, vain or well organized?

6

CONTENTS

CONTENTS

Section 3: LETTER FORMS

GLOSSARY

Angle of writing

Also called the *word slant* or *word tilt*, this is the direction to which letters lean. Letters might be *backward-slanting* (reclined), *forward-slanting* (inclined) or *vertical*.

Angular connecting strokes

When the letters in a *script* are joined together in a sharp, angular way. Compare this to the other types of *connecting stroke*: *arcade*, *garland* and *thread*.

Arcade connecting strokes

When the letters in a *script* are joined together using an umbrella-like, *overhand strok*e. Compare this to the other types of *connecting stroke*: *angular*, *garland* and *thread*.

Ascending baseline

Measured using the *overall baseline*, the lines of text in this type of *baseline slope* rise from the left-hand side of the page to the right-hand side of the page. Compare it to other types of baseline which may be *falsely ascending, descending, concave, convex, level* or *varied.*

Backward-slanting script

Also described as *reclined,* the words in this *script* slant to the left.

Baseline

This is an imaginary line on which letters are written. If the writer is using lined paper, the baseline is the line on which they write. The baseline separates the *middle zone* from the *lower zone*. All lines of text have an *overall baseline* and an *internal baseline.*

Baseline shape

This indicates the degree to which letters in a line of *script* vary about the *overall baseline.* Handwriting often reveals that a baseline may be *rigid, firm, wavering, jumping, sagging* or may be entirely *erratic.*

Baseline slope

This refers to the angle of the *overall baseline,* which may sometimes be level, ascending, falsely ascending, descending, varied, concave, or convex.

Beginning strokes Also called, *starting*, or *pre-strokes*, these are extra *strokes* at the beginning of a word.

Concave baseline Measured using the *overall baseline*, the lines of text in this type of *baseline slope* fall in the middle. Compare it to other types of baseline which may be *ascending, falsely ascending, descending, convex, level* or *varied*.

Connected writing Any type of writing where at least four letters in any word are connected. Compare this to *disconnected writing*.

Connecting strokes The lines that join letters together in *cursive script*. Connecting strokes do not appear in *printed handwriting*. There are four types of connecting stroke: *angular, arcade, garland* and *thread*.

Controlled left slant Handwriting in which the letters slant slightly to the left.

Controlled right slant Handwriting in which the letters slant slightly to the right.

Convex baseline
Measured using the *overall baseline*, the lines of text in this type of *baseline slope* rise in the middle. Compare it to other types of baseline which may be *ascending, falsely ascending, descending, concave, level,* or *varied.*

Cursive script
Script in which the letters are joined, either totally or partially. It is the opposite of printed script.

Degree of slant
The degree to which letters slant forward (to the right) or backward (to the left). Letters within a script might reveal a *controlled, pronounced, extreme,* or even *flattened left* or *right slant*, or they might be *varied* to the left or right or around the vertical.

Descending baseline
Measured using the *overall baseline*, the lines of text in this type of *baseline slope* slant from the top left of the paper to the bottom right of the paper. Compare it to other types of baseline which may be *ascending, falsely ascending,*

concave, *convex*, *level* or
varied.

Disconnected writing   Any type of writing where less
than four letters in any word are
connected. Compare this to
connected writing.

Doodle   Anything scribbled (such as a
face, flower or pattern), often
when the writer was thinking
about something else.

Downstrokes   A mark made by the writing
implement moving from the top
of the paper toward the bottom
of the paper. Downstrokes are
the opposite of *upstrokes*.

End stroke   Also called a *finishing stroke,*
this is the last *stroke* the writer
makes when forming a letter.

Erratic baseline   Text which varies about the
baseline. Compare it to other
baseline shapes such as *firm*,
jumping, *rigid*, *sagging* and
wavering.

Even line spacing   When the space left between
lines of text on a sheet of paper
is regular. Compare this to

narrow, *wide* and *varied line spacing*.

Extreme left slant   Handwriting in which the letters slant markedly to the left but do not actually lie flat.

Extreme right slant   Handwriting in which the letters slant markedly to the right but do not actually lie flat.

Falsely ascending baseline   Measured using the *overall baseline*, the lines of text in this type of *baseline slope* slant from the lower left-hand side of the page to the upper right-hand side and trail off. Compare it to other types of baseline which may be *ascending*, *descending*, *concave*, *convex*, *level* or *varied*.

Fast handwriting   Some graphologists consider handwriting made using more than 200 letters a minute to be fast. It is often characterized by being *garland* in style, sloping to the right, with the *end strokes* of letters often extended to the right, the i-dot and *t-bar* of *lower case letters* appearing to the right of letters.

Finishing stroke

Also called an *end stroke,* this is the last *stroke* the writer makes when forming a letter.

Firm baseline

Text which varies only very little about the *baseline.* Compare it to other *baseline shapes* such as *erratic, jumping, rigid, sagging* and *wavering.*

Flattened left slant

Handwriting in which the letters lie almost completely flat against the baseline having been made to the left. This is the most severe form of leftword-sloping handwriting.

Flattened right slant

Handwriting in which the letters lie almost completely flat against the baseline having been made to the right. This is the most severe form of rightword-sloping handwriting.

Forward-slanting script

Also described as *inclined,* the words in this *script* slant to the right.

Garland connecting strokes

When the letters in a *script* are joined together using a rounded, cup-like, *underhand stroke.* Compare this to the other types of *connecting stroke*: *angular*, *arcade*, and *thread*.

i-dots

Dots made when forming the *lower case letter* "i."

Inlined script

Also described as *forward-slanting script*, the words in this *script* slant to the right.

Internal baseline

An imaginary line which can be drawn beneath the lower part of all *middle zone* letters in a line of *script* and which reveals the *baseline shape*.

Jumping baseline

Text in which a word or a section of an entire line rises above the *baseline*. Compare it to other *baseline shapes* such as *erratic*, *firm*, *rigid*, *sagging* and *wavering*.

Large handwriting

Handwriting is said to be large when the general height of *ascenders* or *descenders* is $^3/_8$" (9mm) or more, or, the overall height of *middle zone letters* is just under $^1/_8$"–about $^3/_{16}$" (2.5mm-4mm).

Left-hand margin

The area left blank between the

far left edge of the handwriting
and the left edge of the paper on
which it is written.

Letter spacing   The amount of space a writer
                        leaves between the letters
                        within words.

Level baseline   Measured using the *overall
                        baseline*, the lines of text in this
                        type of *baseline slope* are
                        horizontal, parallel to the top
                        and bottom of the paper.
                        Compare it to other types of
                        baseline which may be
                        ascending, *falsely ascending*,
                        descending, *concave*, *convex*, or
                        varied.

Line spacing   The space left between lines of
                        text on a sheet of paper. Line
                        spacing may be *even*, *narrow*,
                        wide or *varied*.

Loops   Enclosed parts of a letter. There
                        are u*pper zone loops*, *middle
                        zone loops* and *lower zone
                        loops*.

Lower margin   The area left blank between the
                        bottom of a piece of
                        handwriting and the bottom of

the paper on which it is written.

Lower zone   The area below the *baseline*.

Lower zone loops   Loops that appear in the *lower zone*. Common examples include loops made in the lower case letters f, g, j, q, and y.

Margin   The area left blank between the edge of the handwriting and the paper on which it is written. There are four margins: the *left-hand margin*, the *right-hand margin*, the *upper margin* and the *lower margin*.

Medium-sized handwriting   Handwriting is said to be of medium size when the *ascenders* or *descenders* of *lower case letters* are $1/4$"to $3/8$" (6mm to 9mm) or the overall height of *middle zone letters* is $1/4$"to $3/8$" (1.5 to 2.5mm).

Medium-sized letters   The letters within a sample *script* are considered to be of medium width when the width between *downstrokes* in a single *lower case letter* is more or less equal to the height of that letter.

Middle zone   The area above the *baseline* but
                           below the *upper zone*.

Middle zone letters   Letters that normaly occupy
                           only the *middle zone* because
                           they have no ascenders or
                           descenders. Examples include
                           the letters "o," "a," and "m."

Middle zone loops   Loops that appear in the *middle
                           zone*.

Narrow handwriting   Handwriting is said to be
                           narrow when the width between
                           the *downstrokes* of a single
                           lower case letter in a sample
                           script is less than the height of
                           that letter.

Narrow line spacing   When there is little space left
                           between lines of text on a sheet
                           of paper. Compare this to *even*,
                           wide and *varied line spacing*.

**Narrow word
spacing**   When a writer leaves small
                           spaces between words in a line
                           of text. Some graphologists
                           consider word spacing to be
                           narrow if it is less than the
                           width of the writer's *lower case
                           letter* "n." Compare this to
                           normal and *wide* word spacing.

Normal word spacing   When a writer leaves normal spaces between words in a line of text. Some graphologists consider word spacing to be normal when spaces equal the width of the writer's *lower case letters* "a, e, o or u." Compare this to *narrow* and *wide* word spacing.

Overall baseline   An imaginary line connecting the lower parts of the first and last *middle zone* letters in a line of *script* and which reveals the overall *baseline slope*.

Overhand stroke   *Strokes* made using an umbrella-like shape characteristic of *arcade connections*. Contrast this with the *underhand stroke*.

Perpendicular slant   Also described as *upright* or *vertical slant*, this describes a script in which the words are more or less upright, slanting neither to the left nor to the right. Compare this to *backward* and *forward slanting scripts*.

Pre-strokes   Also called, *beginning*, or

starting strokes, these are extra *strokes* at the beginning of a word.

Printed handwriting   Also known as non-cursive writing. Letters are formed individually and have no connecting *strokes*.

Pronounced left slant   Handwriting in which the letters lean markedly to the left.

Pronounced right slant   Handwriting in which the letters lean markedly to the right.

Reclined script   Also described as *backward-slanting script*, the words in this *script* slant to the left.

Right-hand margin   The area left blank between the far right edge of a piece of handwriting and the right of the paper on which it is written.

Rigid baseline   Text which does not vary about the *baseline*. Compare it to other *baseline shapes* such as *erratic*, *firm*, *jumping*, *sagging* and *wavering*.

Sagging baseline   Text in which a word or a section of an entire line falls

below the *baseline*. Compare it
to other *baseline shapes* such as
erratic, firm, *jumping*, *rigid*,
and *wavering*.

Script   A piece of writing; part of a text
                              or manuscript.

Slow writing   Some graphologists consider
                              handwriting written using less
                              than 100 letters a minute to be
                              slow handwriting. Such writing
                              often demonstrates attention to
                              detail, such as the retouching of
                              strokes.

Small handwriting   Handwriting is considered small
                              if the general height of
                              ascenders or *descenders* in
                              lower case letters is $^1/4$" (6mm)
                              or less, or, the overall height of
                              middle zone letters is less than
                              $^1/16$" (1.5mm).

Spacing   In handwriting analysis this
                              could refer to *letter*, *word* or
                              line spacing.

Starting strokes   Also called, *beginning*, or *pre-
                              strokes*, these are extra *strokes*
                              at the beginning of a word.

Stroke

Shapes formed by the movement of pen across paper. Any individual letter may be made up of several strokes including *pre-strokes* and *end strokes*.

t-bars

Small, horizontal bars used to form part of the *lower case letter* "t."

Thread connecting strokes

When the letters in a *script* are joined together with a thread-like stroke, often making text difficult to read. Compare this to the other types of *connecting stroke*: *angular*, *arcade*, and *garland*.

Underhand stroke

Strokes made using a cup-like shape characteristic of *garland connecting strokes*. Contrast this with the *overhand stroke*.

Upper margin

The area left blank between the top of a piece of handwriting and the top of the paper on which it is written.

Upper zone

The area above the *middle zone*.

Upper zone loops

Loops that appear in the *upper*

zone. Common examples include loops made in the lower case letters b, d, f, h, and l.

Upright slant Also described as *perpendicular* or *vertical slant*, this describes a script in which the words are more or less upright, slanting neither to the left nor to the right. Compare this to *backward* and *forward slanting scripts*.

Upstrokes A mark made by the writing implement moving from the bottom of the paper toward the top of the paper. Upstrokes are opposite to *downstrokes*.

Varied baseline Measured using the *overall baseline*, the lines of text in this type of *baseline slope* vary. They might be *ascending*, *falsely ascending*, *descending*, *concave*, *convex*, or *level*.

Varied line spacing When the space left between lines of text on a sheet of paper is irregular. Compare this to *even*, *narrow*, and *wide line spacing*.

Varied word slant Handwriting which varies either

to the right and left, or which varies in the degree to which it slopes either to the right or left.

Vertical slant Also described as *perpendicular* or *upright slant*, this describes a script in which the words are more or less upright, slanting neither to the left nor to the right. Compare this to *backward* and *forward-slanting scripts*.

Wide letters Individual letters within a sample *script* are considered to be wide when the width between *downstrokes* in a single letter is greater than the height of that letter.

Wide line spacing When there is much space left between lines of text on a sheet of paper. Compare this to *even*, *narrow*, and *varied line spacing*.

Wide word spacing Large spaces left between words in a line of text. Some graphologists consider *word spacing* to be wide if it is greater than the width of the writer's *lower case letter* "w."

Word slant

Compare this to *narrow* and *normal* word spacing.
Also called the *angle of writing* or *word tilt*, this is the direction to which letters lean. Letters might be *backward-slanting* (reclined), *forward-slanting* (inclined) or *vertical*.

Word spacing

The amount of space a writer leaves between words in a line of text. Word spacing may be *narrow*, *normal* or *wide*.

Word tilt

Also called the *angle of writing* or *word slant*, this is the direction to which letters lean. Letters might be *backward-slanting* (reclined), *forward-slanting* (inclined) or *vertical*.

Section 1
GETTING
STARTED

Graphology defined
Grapho is the Greek for *writing*, and *logy*
means *study*. So, graphology is the study of
handwriting, and in particular in order to reveal
character and personality traits.

Part of the first draft of the Declaration of
Independence in the hand of Thomas Jefferson.
The revisions are in the handwriting of
Benjamin Franklin and John Adams.

1

This section will give you a thorough grounding in the history and basic principles of graphology, provide an introduction to the various uses of graphology, and explain how to get started in the study of graphology.

How this section is organized
- **HISTORY OF GRAPHOLOGY**
- **WHY ANALYZE HANDWRITING?**
- **GRAPHOTHERAPY**
- **FORENSIC GRAPHOLOGY**
- **THE BASICS**
- **HOW TO USE THIS BOOK**

HISTORY OF GRAPHOLOGY

Ancient origins
You could be forgiven for thinking that graphology was a relatively new science. In fact, it has a history stretching back centuries. Six thousand years ago, the ancient Chinese were already analyzing their calligraphy, assessing it for revealed personality traits. In Europe a few thousand years later, in ancient Greece and Rome, handwriting analysis was being carried out to high levels. The ancient Greek philosopher Aristotle (384–322 B.C.) is quoted as saying:

Aristotle

"Spoken words are the symbols of mental experience, and written words are the symbols of spoken words."

Suetonius (c. A.D. 69–140), a Roman historian, included handwriting analyses in his celebrated work, *Lives of the Caesars.*

Monkish roots
Monks in the Middle Ages also studied how handwriting reveals character, and in 1622 Italian physician Camille Baldo (or Baldi) wrote the first known work on graphology.

It was a 19th-century monk, however, who really put graphology on the map. The term *graphology* was coined by the Frenchman Abbé Jean-Hippolyte Michon (1806–1881). Michon collected and studied thousands of handwriting samples, eventually publishing an account of his system of analysis.

German influences

Nineteenth-century German graphologists such as Dr. Ludwig Klages (1872–1956) made great advances in the systemization of graphology. Klages created a systematic theory linking handwriting with personality. He established links between graphology and more accepted sciences such as psychology and physiology. Under his influence, graphology made the first steps toward being viewed as a science rather than an art.

Graphology today

Michon and Klages are often seen as the founding fathers of modern graphology, yet there have been many since them who have contributed to this discipline. Today, graphology is often studied in universities and colleges, and is frequently a part of psychology courses.

WHY ANALYZE HANDWRITING?

Why would you want to analyze someone's
handwriting? The answer is that you want to know
something about that person's character — sometimes
things that they would not, perhaps, tell you or even be
sure of themselves. Graphology can be used as a tool to
assess yourself, friends, or even complete strangers.

There are only six recognized versions of Shakespeare
signature (above), but many forged ones.

Basic principles of graphology

- Although they may be similar, no two handwritings
  are identical. Each person's handwriting is
  unique and therefore provides an insight into his or
  her individual character.

- Graphology cannot be used to reveal the age or sex of
  an individual. Handwriting can reveal masculine or
  feminine character, and maturity and immaturity,
  since these can be present in the handwriting of
  someone no matter the gender or age.

- Graphology cannot be used to predict the future; it is
  not a crystal ball.

President J.F. Kennedy was well known for signing his signature in different styles.

How can I use graphology?
Graphology can be used in a variety of situations:

- **Psychologists** often study graphology so that they can use this as another character-analysis tool for studying human behavior.

- **Graphotherapists** believe it can even be used to assess and improve the state of a person's mental health.

- **Graphopathologists** believe handwriting can be used as medical diagnostic tool, identifying the particular disease or condition a writer has. While graphopathology has largely fallen out of favor, it is now accepted that handwriting analysis can provide warning signs of an illness in the early stages.

- **Forensic graphologists** are employed to check the veracity of documents, to see if a signature or other writing has been forged, and to identify, or not, suspects by their handwriting.

Eleven applicants for the same job; their signatures are reproduced to a common scale:

Yours sincerely, *David Owen   Peter Cassidy*

Caroline Smith   Peter J Marryon

Matthew Tanner.   Joy Tucker!

Will Hoare   Robert Hayman   Philip Scott

Sally Henry   Ravesdge

- **Personnel departments** often employ graphologists to assess job and promotion applicants. A trained graphologist can save a company hundreds of dollars that would otherwise be wasted in expensive interviews or inappropriate selections. If you are applying for a job, and are required to write something by hand, don't try to cheat by altering your handwriting. A good graphologist will be able to spot someone who is doctoring his handwriting. Graphological tests have even been designed to test an applicant's I.Q.

- **Hobbyists** take up graphology as a tool to learn more about themselves and their friends or family. Some might just use it as entertainment at parties. If you are such a one, remember to only ever analyze a sample of writing that has been voluntarily given. Limit yourself to positive comments at parties, and give each analysis a time limit of, say, 10 minutes.

- **Counselors** can use graphology to advise people on compatibility or help assess a personal relationship.

How does handwriting reveal someone's character?
Handwriting reveals character in a variety of ways, each of which is covered in more detail in the rest of this book. How writers form letters, the strokes they use, the general style of writing and so on all provide the graphologist with clues.

For heAVEN S
SARe @Atc h me
Before 1 Rill more
I eANNot eamjrol myself

A Chicago serial killer's appeal for help, written on the wall of the bedroom of one of his victims.

Why does handwriting reveal someone's character?
Physical movement is an expression of personality, and handwriting is a particularly unique sort of movement for which fine motor skills and great concentration are required. Graphologists sometimes talk of handwriting as being brainwriting, since it is such a good mirror of a person's thoughts, both conscious and subconscious.

GRAPHOTHERAPY

Graphology can not only reveal character traits, but many people believe it can also help you to improve on the negative ones. Graphotherapy is the use of graphological skills to remedy character faults and weaknesses and strengthen positive attributes.

History
The term graphotherapy was first used in 1930s France by the psychologist Dr. Edgar Berillon. Others tested his theories at the famous Sorbonne University in Paris, France, and their results seemed to support his findings. More recently, two famous U.S. graphotherapists, Paul de Sainte Colombe and Kathi Lanier de Sainte Colombe, published a seminal text: *Grapho-Therapeutics*.

Theory
The theory behind graphotherapy is that in the same way your thoughts and moods affect your handwriting, the way you write has an impact on the way you feel and think. Therefore, by changing the way you write you can change the way you think.

How to carry out graphotherapy
Only a trained and experienced graphologist and graphotherapist should carry out graphotherapy on another person. If you wish to try it for yourself, however, follow these steps:

1 Make a complete character analysis based on
  handwriting samples.

2 Tackling one trait at a time, identify a single problem area that you want to change, using your own knowledge of your character and life history to pinpoint the problem area.

3 Get a friend or colleague who knows you well to look over the results and make sure you are being honest with yourself.

4 Design a positive statement about the trait you want to change. For example, if you wanted tackle a lack of confidence, the sentence could be:

I am in control of my life, and have nothing to fear

This insecurity could be revealed by a left-ward slant in your handwriting.

5 Choose a comfortable place to sit, find your favorite writing implements and schedule a regular time to carry out the therapy.

6 Write the sentence at least 10 times on one piece of paper, trying to write in a more vertical style, in this case. Date the paper and keep it in a file.

7 Repeat the practice session twice a day, and monitor any changes in your handwriting over time by comparing the dated sheets.

What you should notice over a period of time, is that the trait corrects itself in both your handwriting and your behavior.

FORENSIC GRAPHOLOGY

Forensic graphologists will be asked to identify forged handwriting and match handwriting samples, often in the detection of crimes.

Forged signatures
A common task is checking the veracity of signatures, on suspect wills or checks, for example.

In these two examples, signatures **a** are verified samples of an authentic signature. Either signatures **b** or **c** are real ones and the others are forgeries.
Can you tell which is the forgery?

a   With best wishes,

Melissa Hixon

b   With best wishes.

                     c   With best wishes.

a Best regards,

Richard Hummerstone

b Best regards,

c Best regards,

The answer is signature **c** in the first example and signature **b** in the second.

Indicators in the forgeries include:

- Heavier pressure, produced by the greater concentration needed by the forger to write the signature
- The letters are more carefully formed: it is difficult to forge a quickly written signature well and maintain an impression of speed.
- Note that in the second example it was easier for the forger to get it right because the real signator has rounded, disconnected letters that gave the forger time to take more care.

THE BASICS

You do not need any special equipment for graphology,
only some samples of handwriting.

Collecting samples
You can start exploring graphology by using any
samples of handwriting that you can lay your hands on.
As you get more experienced, however, you will need
to be more rigorous about how you collect samples.

Points to remember include:

- Samples must be written in script, not printed.
- Try to get samples from the same person written on
  both lined and unlined paper.
- Ask subjects to use a ballpoint pen; but also try to
  find out what sort of pen they prefer to use normally.
- Get a signature on each sample, as signatures can be
  very revealing. But also ask them to print their name
  in case the signature is illegible.

- Some graphologists devise a set question that the subjects write out. Others prefer to ask people to just write 100 words about what ever they wish, arguing that this gives a more natural sample. Perhaps the best solution is to request letters and documents already in existence, as these will provide the most natural examples of writing style. Any sample of handwriting written specifically for an analysis may be warped by the writer's knowledge of its impending use.
- Try to collect more than one sample per person, preferably written under different circumstances. This will enable you to isolate rogue indicators from more regularly occurring indicators.

WARNINGS
- Absence of an indicator has no meaning at all.
- A person's handwriting can vary. It can be affected by illness or worry, for example, and for this reason it would be unwise for you to over-simplify your analysis or to make an analysis based on one sample of handwriting.
- Never look at one indicator in isolation. Before you assume that a person has a certain personality trait based on one indicator in the text, make sure it is backed up by at least one other indicator. This principle is so important to successful graphology that you will find it repeated throughout the book.
- The indicators and what they reveal as discussed in this book only apply to adults. Do not apply the same rules to children. The handwriting of juveniles often has indicators that would be very worrying if seen in an adult's script — mostly with no cause for alarm.

HOW TO USE THIS BOOK

You can access the information in this book
in a variety of ways:

- You can look at a particular handwriting trait on
  its own, for example, analyze the word slant or
  baseline. Then combine the analyses to get a
  complete picture of the subject.

- Alternatively, you can look up a particular character
  trait (in the index; in the A-Z of letter forms; or in the
  following list) and find out what signs to look for in
  the handwriting. You might want to do this if, for
  example, you had to decide which sample of
  handwriting from a selection revealed an
  aggressive nature.

- Alternatively, you can just read the book, teaching
  yourself graphology as you go.

A 19th-century game of making patterns by folding and
pressing a signature while the ink is still wet.

Character traits

The following section tells you which parts of your handwriting are used to identify particular *character traits* or personality types. The letters in SMALL CAPITALS indicate which part to look up in the contents:

Character traits	Part to look up
ability to prepare themselves for a job of work	STARTING STROKES
adaptability, sociability, and attitude toward other people	SPACING used between letters, words and lines.
attitude of the writer toward others	CONNECTING STROKES
attitudes based on past experience	END STROKES
attitudes to the future	the BASELINE, the size of the MARGINS
attitudes to the past	the BASELINE, the size of the MARGINS
attitudes to the present	the BASELINE
capacity for concentration	the SIZE of letters
confidence in ability to make decisions	the BASELINE
	continued overleaf

Character traits	Part to look up
confidence in ability to succeed	the BASELINE
current behavior of the writer	END STROKES
degree of determination	the evenness of PRESSURE used
degree to which writer communicates feelings to others	WORD SLANT
depth of emotional responses	SPEED of handwriting
desires	the PRESSURE used
grasp of new situations	STARTING STROKES
how writer adapts to his or her environment	END STROKES, SIZE: the height and width of letters
how writer feels life is likely to treat him or her	the BASELINE
importance placed on the past	STARTING STROKES
intellectual abilities	SPEED of handwriting
intensity felt for certain words and phrases	the PRESSURE used
introversion and extroversion	the SIZE of letters

Character traits	Part to look up
lifestyle writer prefers	the HEIGHT of letters
mental energy writer puts into reaching his or her goals	the BASELINE
need for personal space	the WIDTH of letters
need to draw attention	STARTING STROKES
personal vitality	PRESSURE used
personality traits	DOODLES
physical vitality	the PRESSURE used
planning ability	variations between the left and right, and top and bottom MARGINS
preferences	the PRESSURE used
public self-image	the SIGNATURE
relationships	the width of a MARGIN
self-expression	the SIZE of letters
social attitude of the writer	END STROKES
speed of physical reactions	SPEED of handwriting
speed of thoughts	SPEED of handwriting

Section 2
THINGS TO INVESTIGATE

What does a graphologist look for?
Graphologists consider style elements, such as
speed, spacing, pressure, and letter strokes alongside
factors such as what type of pen, paper, and ink was
used as well as how they address an envelope. While
you can consult each part alone to study one particular
aspect, remember that one indicator by itself is not
enough to consider that person to be in possession of
the trait.

How this chapter is organized
This section is arranged into twenty parts:
- BASELINES examines how people keep to the line.
- CONNECTING STROKES looks at the way that
  writers connect letters.
- DOODLES tells you what those seemingly
  meaningless scribbles we do really mean.
- END STROKES shows you how to read
  what is indicated by how the writer forms
  the last stroke of a letter.
- ENVELOPES reveals how signifigant the
  addressing of an envelope is.
- INK tells you what it means if a writer
  chooses a particular color of ink.

2

- LOOPS teaches you what to look for in the way a person forms ascenders and descenders.
- LEFT-HANDEDNESS is an important factor to consider when analyzing someone's writing.
- MARGINS looks at how lines are placed on the page.
- NUMERALS studies how digits can reveal truths.
- PAPER classifies the different paper types and tells you what they reveal.
- PRESSURE sets out how to evaluate the writing pressure and what different pressures reveal.
- SIGNATURES deals with some of the most revealing words people write—their own names.
- SIZE asseses the importance of how big a person's writing is.
- SPACING is analyzed in this part.
- SPEED shows what the pace of writing reveals.
- STARTING STROKES looks at how writers make the first stroke of a letter.
- WORD SLANT helps you assess and evaluate the direction and degree of "lean" in handwriting.
- WRITING TOOLS helps you recognize and evaluate the use of different pens and pencils.
- ZONES analyzes the three zones that letters use: upper, middle, and lower.

BASELINES

The baseline is that part of the writing which rests on the line if a writer is using lined paper. Descenders (the loops of lowercase letters "**f**", "**g**", "**j**", "**q**" and "**y**") normally fall below the baseline.

> This is the baseline.
> Loops of f, g, j, q, and
> y fall beneath it.

What does the baseline tell you?
- the writer's attitudes about the past, present, and future
- the mental energy a writer puts into reaching his or her goals
- the writer's confidence in his or her ability to make decisions
- the writer's confidence in his or her ability to succeed
- how the writer feels life is likely to treat him or her

Measuring the baseline
There are two aspects to consider when measuring baselines: their *slope* and their *shape*.
The slope of the baseline depends on whether it runs parallel with the top and bottom of the writing page.

Baselines may be horizontal or may slope upward or downward; they may be convex or concave, or they may be erratic.

The shape of the baseline depends on whether the baselines of a line of script (the internal baseline) waver from the overall baseline.

To measure the overall baseline, put a sheet of tracing paper over your sample handwriting and, using a ruler, join the first and last letters of a line of script.

The overall baseline. overall
baseline

To measure the internal baseline, draw a dotted line connecting the lower part of middle-case letters.

The overall baseline
internal baseline

How to use this section
Using several samples of the same person's handwriting, measure the overall and internal baselines and compare them to the examples shown here. Remember to take into account other factors of your handwriting analysis when making your assessment.

SLOPE OF BASELINE

Level baseline

- controls moods
- even-tempered
- level-headed
- stable
- reasonable
- reliable
- realistic
- well-organized

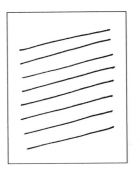

Ascending baseline

- ambitious
- energetic
- excited
- has faith in the future
- invigorated
- involved in many activities simultaneously
- joyful
- may be unrealistic
- optimistic
- wants to stay busy

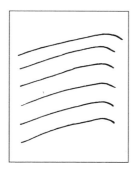

Falsely ascending baseline

- a quitter.

The point at which the lines begin to fall indicates that point in a project's progress at which the writer quits.

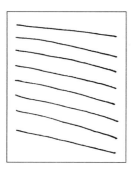

Descending baseline

- critical
- depressed
- discouraged
- fatalist
- fatigued
- pessimist
- tired
- unwell
- weak

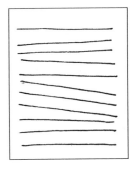

Varied baseline

- moody
- temperamental

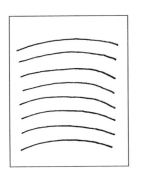

Convex baseline

- a brilliant starter
- begins projects enthusiastically and optimistically but tires and may not finish

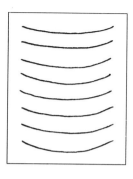

Concave baseline

- a reliable finisher
- likes beginnings and endings
- lacks initial confidence but overcomes negativity and eventually becomes positive

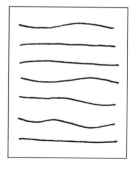

Baseline falls and rises more than once

- battles against continuous discouragement

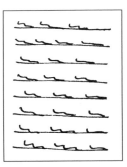

Constant baselines, descending words

- fights depression and lack of self-confidence

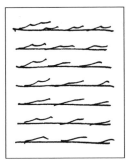

Constant baselines, ascending words

- enthusiastic
- lacks stamina
- over-optimistic attitude to life

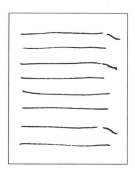

Suicidal baselines

- someone with suicidal tendencies
- may give up suddenly and unexpectedly

SHAPE OF BASELINE

Rigid
straight, like a line of type

This is a rigid baseline

- good decision-maker
- never self-doubting
- does not permit him- or herself to be wrong

Firm
fairly straight, slight or occasional irregularity

This is a steady baseline

- can visualize goals
- occasional self-doubts

Wavering
some letters dip below the line

This is a wavering baseline

- can visualize goals
- has occasional self-doubts

some letters float above the line

This is a wavering baseline

- conflict with established guidelines
- doubts goals, lifestyle, or profession

Jumping
section of a line or an entire word jumps above the line

It was great to see you!

• a moment of elation
Raised words suggest happiness; the more, the happier the writer is

Sagging
section of a line or an entire word sags below the line

I felt bad about it.

• a moment of unhappiness or depression
Sagged words suggest depression; the more often they occur, the more depressed the writer

Erratic

I feelt really confused by it

• confusion
• emotional ups and downs

• insecurity
• self-doubt

CONNECTING STROKES

Connecting strokes are the lines that join letters
together in cursive script. There are no connecting
strokes in the handwriting samples of people who print
their words.

What do connecting strokes reveal?
Connecting strokes reveal the attitude of the writer
toward others.

Types
There are four types of connecting stroke: arcades,
garlands, threads, and angles. Most people use a
combination of connecting strokes, with one of the
above methods predominating.

How to use this section
Identify which type of connecting strokes — angular,
arcade, garland, or thread — are used by the writer
of your handwriting sample. Decide which
predominates, then read about the suggested
character traits on the pages that follow. Add these
character traits to what you have already discovered
about your subject. Read also about the differences
between connected and disconnected writing at the
end of this section. Decide whether the sample you
have to analyze is characteristic of your subject or
whether you need additional samples. Remember,
handwriting varies and it is always advisable to have
more than one sample.

Angular
Letters are connected using angles.

M = _M_   n = _n_

- aggressive
- cold
- competitive
- conscientious
- conventional
- decisive
- determined
- disciplined
- dissatisfied
- domineering
- egotistical
- energetic
- enthusiastic
- excitable
- firm
- goal-orientated
- hardworking
- idealistic
- initiating
- intolerant
- irritable
- logical
- persistent
- quarrelsome
- reliable
- rigid
- slow
- strict
- strong-minded
- stubborn
- suspicious
- tense
- thorough
- uncompromising
- unsociable
- unyielding

Garland

As taught in most Western schools, letters are connected using a rounded, cup-like, underhand stroke. The deeper the garland (or "cup"), the more receptive the writer. Sham garlands are when the writer makes certain lowercase letters look like other lowercase letters: an "**m**" is made to look like a "**w**", a "**w**" looks like an "**m**", a "**u**" looks like an "**n**", and an "**n**" looks like a "**u**".

Deep garland

Shallow garland

- adaptable
- affectionate
- avoids conflict
- careless
- confident
- fickle
- flexible
- friendly
- good communicator
- good listener
- hospitable
- indolent
- informal
- kind
- lacking self-discipline
- lazy
- natural
- open to influence
- outgoing
- peace-loving
- receptive
- responsive
- sincere
- spontaneous
- superficial
- sympathetic
- tactless
- talkative
- thoughtless
- tolerant
- uncalculating
- warm

- contemplative
- depressed
- feels deeply for others
- sympathetic

- amiable
- elusive
- obliging
- reckless
- superficial
- unrestrained

Threads

Letters are connected with almost flattened thread-like lines, usually making words difficult to read.

Arcade

Letters are connected using an umbrella-like, overhand stroke. The flatter the arcade, the more the writer tries to cover things up. The higher the arcade, the more artistic the writer is likely to be.

Flat arcades

- adaptable
- changeable
- clever
- creative
- deceitful
- diplomatic
- easily influenced
- elusive
- insincere
- instinctive
- intelligent
- intuitive
- lacking conscience
- lacking stamina
- manipulative
- opportunistic
- perceptive
- rebellious
- resentful
- spontaneous
- talented
- versatile

- altruistic
- artistic
- balanced
- bigoted
- deceptive
- desire to cover up
- desire to control
- diplomatic
- dissembling
- emotionally isolated
- formal
- concerned with appearances
- hypocritical
- independent
- individualistic
- inscrutable
- kind
- lacking spontaneity
- meditative
- modest
- protective
- proud
- reserved
- scheming
- secretive
- shy
- trustworthy

- defensive
- hypocritical
- pretentious
- secretive

CONNECTED AND DISCONNECTED WRITING

Connected writing
Letters are connected in a progressive movement.

Whole words connected

Disconnected writing
Letters are not connected.

Combination of connected and disconnected script

Disconnected first letters

Disconnected last letters

- adjustable
- cooperative
- dependent
- good memory
- lacking initiative

- logical
- organized
- persistent
- systematic thinker
- tenacious

- highly creative, intelligent, and logical with a fondness for solving problems

---

- detached
- individualistic
- intuitive
- inventive

- isolated
- observant
- poor adaptor
- unsociable

- creative
- independent
- intelligent
- intuitive

- occasionally irritated
- sensitive
- tense

- cautious
- observant
- procrastinating

- ambivalent
- hesitant
- reflective of decisions

DOODLES

Doodles are images of anything – scribbled often, when thinking about something else.

What do doodles reveal?

Doodles can reveal personality traits. Because they are usually made unconsciously they can reveal the writer's ambitions, anxieties, desires, and fears. In psycho-analysis doodles are often used for assessing personality.

Things to look for when analyzing doodles

- the writing implement used
- the position of the doodle on the page
- type of lines used
- size of doodle
- pressure and shading used
- the type of doodle

WRITING IMPLEMENT USED

Usually people doodle with whatever writing implement they happen to have at hand at the time, and do not deliberately select an implement in order to doodle. See the section on writing implements for more information about the character traits the doodles reveal.

POSITION ON THE PAGE

The page on which a doodle is drawn may be divided
into three horizontal zones and three vertical zones.

Position on page	Indicates
Left of page 	• past • introversion • self • mother
Right of page 	• future • extroversion • others • father
Center page 	• present

Position of doodle	**Corresponds with**
Horizontal upper zone 	upper zone writing: • the superego or conscience • the future • the upper body
Horizontal middle zone 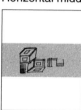	middle zone writing: • the ego • the present • the middle body
Horizontal lower zone 	lower zone writing: • the id, which includes the libido • the past • the lower body

TYPE OF LINES USED

Line	Indicates
Curved 	These have the same meanings as curved strokes used in handwriting: • affection • flexibility • kindness • love
Wavy lines 	Common among actors, dancers, and singers. • affection • kindness • love • love of movement
Spikes 	• aggression • antisocial behaviour • hostility • violence

Line	Indicates
Straight	● aggression ● constructiveness ● criticism ● self-reliance

Straight lines that are complicated	● aggression ● constructiveness ● criticism ● determination ● intensity ● self-reliance

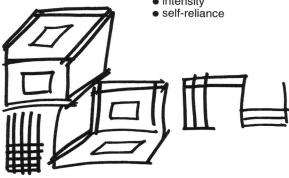

SIZE OF DOODLE

The size of the doodle is often a measure of the doodler's self-esteem.

Large doodles may indicate ambition and a strong ego.

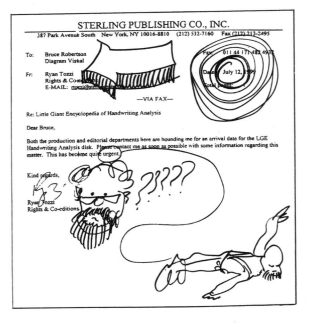

STERLING PUBLISHING CO., INC.

387 Park Avenue South   New York, NY 10016-8810   (212) 532-7160   Fax (212) 213-2495

To: Bruce Robertson
      Diagram Vistal

Fr: Ryan Tozzi
      Rights & Co-editions
      E-MAIL: rtozzi@sterlingpub.com

Fax: 011 44 171 481 4935

Date: July 12, 1999

Total pages:

—VIA FAX—

Re: Little Giant Encyclopedia of Handwriting Analysis

Dear Bruce,

Both the production and editorial departments here are hounding me for an arrival date for the LGE Handwriting Analysis disk. Please contact me as soon as possible with some information regarding this matter. This has become quite urgent.

Kind regards,

Ryan Tozzi
Rights & Co-editions

Large and complicated doodles suggest someone artistic, highly creative, and with initiative.

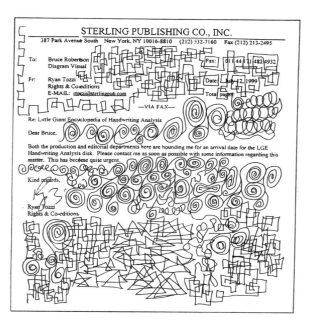

Small doodles suggest a lack of self-esteem.

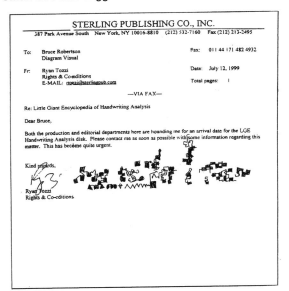

PRESSURE AND SHADING USED

It is not always possible to evaluate the type of pressure used by a doodler, as certain writing implements are less revealing of pressure than others: fiber-tipped pens make analysis of pressure particularly difficult, for example. In general, the greater the pressure used when doodling, the more the doodler is repressing his or her anger.

Pressure	Indicates
Heavy	• anger • determination • intensity • sadness • seriousness
Light	• acceptance • forgiveness • friendliness • sensitivity
Shading	• anxiety • apprehension • deviousness • fear • tension • worry • may also reveal that the writer feels trapped The doodler is likely to have felt greater anxiety and tension when doodling image (**a**) than when doodling image (**b**).

TYPES OF DOODLE

AEROPLANES

- adventurous
- likes travel

ANIMALS

(*See also* birds, cats, crocodiles, fish, furry animals, and snakes.) In general, animals indicate

- a love of the outdoors
- a love of those smaller and weaker than the doodler.

ARROWS

- aggressive
- antisocial
- hostile
- sadistic tendencies
- violent

BIRDS

- affectionate
- considerate
- gentle
- loves freedom
- loves the outdoors

BODY PARTS

(*See also* eyes, faces, lips, and feet.) Doodling a body part suggests a preoccupation with that part of the body, perhaps as a result of illness or because that part is prominent.

BOXES

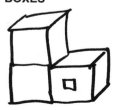

- constructive-minded
- emotionally trapped
- feels claustrophobic
- clear ambitions and goals
- head rules heart
- intellectual

Boxes slanted to the right

- extrovert
- open to new ideas
- progressive

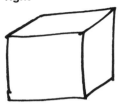

Boxes slanted to the left

- cautious
- hesitant
- secretive

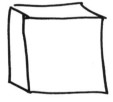

Boxes slanted both left and right

- inconsistent
- versatile

BRACKETS

- likes facts and solving problems

 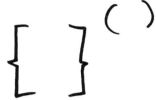

CANDLES

- preoccupation with eroticism

CARS

- adventurous
- likes travel

CATS

- affectionate
- daydreamer
- gullible
- sentimental
- unrealistic

Cats curled

- need for security

CHECK MARKS

- needs encouragement in order to succeed
- skeptical

CHURCH SPIRES

- preoccupation with eroticism

CIRCLES

- affectionate
- kind
- loves harmony
- loving
- needs to give and receive love
- sensitive
- unaggressive

CROCODILES

- preoccupation with sex

DAGGERS AND KNIVES

- aggressive
- antisocial
- hostile
- violent

EYES

- an interest in that part of the body
- clever
- hostile
- resentful
- suspicious

Attractive eyes

- loves and is impressed by beauty

FACES
Face turned to the left of the page

Faces provide clues to how the writer reacts to other people, whether he or she is reserved and shy, or sociable.

- difficulty establishing friendships
- introspective
- slightly reserved or shy

Face turned to the right of the page

- creative
- impulsive
- forward-thinking
- unaware of the feelings of others

Full face

- friendly
- mixes easily
- sociable

Thin face

- inhibited
- lacking warmth
- repressed

Unhappy face

- angry
- dislike of self
- dissatisfied
- fear
- paranoia
- resentful
- frustrated
- unhappy

Ugly face

- angry
- dislike of self
- dissatisfied
- fear
- frustrated
- paranoia
- resentful
- unhappy

Distorted features

- angry
- frustrated
- unhappy

Smiling face

- affectionate
- happy
- content

Face wearing glasses

- concealing a secret

Face with mustache   ● concealing a secret

Face with pipe   ● aggressive
                                  ● angry

Face with cigar   ● aggressive
                                  ● angry

Face with teeth showing
- frustration
- sexual anxiety

Face with tightly sealed lips
- emotionally withdrawn
- inhibited

Face with generous lips
- loving
- warm

Face with long eyelashes

Often drawn by teenage girls wanting to appear glamorous

Many faces

- gregarious
- need for social life

Adding glasses, a mustache, or a beard to an already finished image

This suggests someone who desires authority but has very little.

FEET
Tiny feet

● insecurity

FISH

● preoccupation with sex

FLOWERS

● affectionate
● compassionate
● daydreamer
● gullible
● kind
● loving
● sentimental
● unrealistic
● warmhearted

FURRY ANIMALS

- avoids conflict
- emotional
- gullible
- kind
- sentimental
- tries to maintain harmony
- unaggressive

GALLOWS

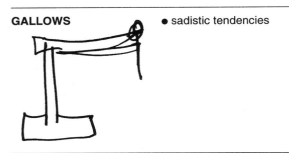

- sadistic tendencies

GUNS

- aggressive
- antisocial
- hostile
- violent

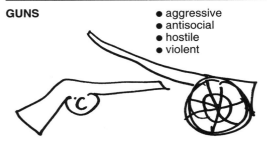

HEARTS

- affectionate
- compassionate
- daydreamer
- gullible
- loving
- kind
- sentimental
- unrealistic
- warmhearted

HOUSES
House with smoke
coming from chimney

- affectionate
- compassionate
- need for family, home, and security
- unambitious
- warmhearted

House without doors or
windows

- inhibited
- lacking warmth
- repressed

LEAVES

- affectionate
- kind
- loving

LETTERS
Odd- shaped letters
(especially "B" and
"W")

- preoccupation with eroticism

Initials entwined

- affectionate
- compassionate
- warmhearted

DOODLES

Letters slanted to the right

- extrovert
- open to new ideas
- progressive

Letters slanted to the left

- cautious
- hesitant
- secretive

Letters slanted to both the left and right

- inconsistent behavior
- versatile

LIPS

- preoccupation with lips themselves
- preoccupation with eroticism

MAZES

- baffled
- feels caught
- frustrated
- seeking to find a solution to a problem
- worried

MONEY
(dollar or pound sign)

- obsessed with money

NUMBERS

If repeated, preoccupation with figures and money

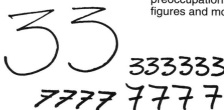

PLANTS

- affectionate
- compassionate
- kind
- loving
- warmhearted

PEOPLE
Thin figure

- inhibited
- lacking warmth
- repressed

Toothpick-type people

These often include the physical characteristics of the doodler and are therefore a representation of the doodler themselves.

A person crossed out

- fussy
- doodler feels like crossing him- or herself out

REPETITIVE DOODLING (commonly use of figure 8)

- careful
- cautious
- consistent
- down-to-earth
- logical
- loving
- loyal
- obsessional
- practical
- timid

ROADS
Complicated
interchanges

- a good problem solver
- likes details
- logical
- reasonable

ROPE

- aggressive
- antisocial
- hostile
- sadistic tendencies
- violent

SHIPS

- adventurous
- likes travel

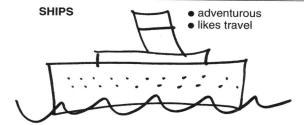

SHOES
- preoccupation with eroticism

SNAKES
- preoccupation with sex

SPIRALS
Decreasing ovals
- fears taking risks
- repressed

SQUARES

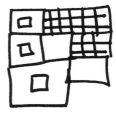

- clear ambitions and goals
- constructive-minded
- emotionally trapped
- feels claustrophobic
- head rules heart

SUN

This is a positive image.
- adaptable
- sensitive

TIC-TAC-TOE

- a planner
- likes competition

TREES
Tree with spikes

- bitter
- inhibited
- lacking warmth
- orderly
- repressed
- sarcastic
- strong-willed
- stubborn
- tense

Tree with fluffy outline

- active
- friendly
- kind
- romantic
- sociable
- superficial
- unaggressive

Tree with leaves

- affectionate
- compassionate
- warmhearted

Tree with fruit

- affectionate
- compassionate
- warmhearted

WEAPONS

- aggressive
- antisocial
- hostile
- violent

WEBS

- baffled
- feels caught
- frustrated
- seeking to find a
  solution to a problem
- worried

DOODLE SELF-ANALYSIS

The following exercise will give you a chance to
analyze your own doodles. This exercise is just part of
a specially designed test that is used in many countries
to assess different aspects of someone's personality.

How to do the doodle test
Take a pen and paper and trace the square
with the circle inside.

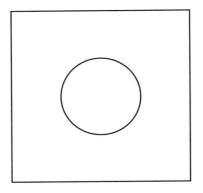

Now, inside the box draw the first thing
that comes into your head.

If you were doing the full doodle test, you
would be asked to do the same for 12 different
boxes in all. Each box would have a different
shape or pattern inside it, as below.

What does the doodle test reveal?

What you have drawn is what is called a conscious doodle—a doodle drawn for a purpose, as it were, not not simply to wile away the time or relieve boredom, which is why most doodles are drawn.

If you were "honest" and really drew the first image that came into your head, the resulting doodle can be very revealing of your hopes, ambitions, state of mind, and your self-image.

Look for the cateogory description and doodle nearest to your doodle, and see what it tells you about yourself:

FACES
simply drawn, often disembodied
To turn the circle into a face is one of the most frequent responses. Such doodles, if drawn simply, are normally quite straightforward to analyze: a happy face is a happy doodler; a sad face is a sad doodler, and so on.

Carefully drawn faces

If the doodle is slightly more elaborate, however, with greater care taken to impart some sort of personality to the doodled face, the doodle is not quite so straightforward. It can either represent:

● how the doodler would like to be seen, or

● how the doodler perceives him or herself.

This doodled face has a downcast look to it. While quite detailed and showing little white space in the face, the doodle seems to have been hastily drawn.

● poor self image, of which they may not even be aware.

This doodled face has lots of white space. The face is smiling, and the teeth are showing.

- wants to be thought of as confident

face scribbled out

This can be a bad sign. A lot depends, however, on the amount of pressure used. In general, it means that the doodler harbors self-destructive or negative feelings.

- self-critical (if pressure is slight)

● depressed and self-hating (if pressure is heavy)

man drawing a woman's face, or woman drawing a man's face

● confused about their masculinity (if a man)
● confused about their femininity (if a woman)

SUN

Turning the circle into the Sun is also one of the most
common responses. Factors to consider include how
the rays are drawn and symmetry.

symmetrical rays

- balanced and calm
- perfectionist
- has a sense of purpose

asymmetrical rays

- troubled mentally
- emotional

FLOWER

- underestimates his or her strengths

DRAWING OUTSIDE THE BOX

- sees him or herself as a rebel
- a person of frustrated ambitions

CIRCLE FILLED IN

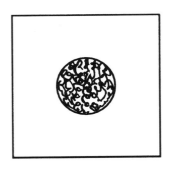

- perhaps suicidal
- vindictive
- passive-aggresive

LANDSCAPE

- hides behind self-confident exterior
- if circle is the moon, the person sees themselves as creative

FIGURE OF EIGHT
extra loop added beneath circle

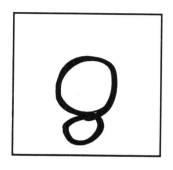

- likes to be seen as the devil's advocate

loop added to top of circle

- has an overly high self-image
- feels awkward sometimes

SNOWMAN

- ingratiating
- seeks contentment

SQUARE FILLED IN

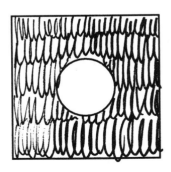

- challenging
- has a unique perspective on life
- noncomformist
- has a positive outlook on the future

ABSTRACT

- has high ambitions
- realistic self image
- contemplative

CONVOLUTED

- unconcerned about the opinions of others
- intellectual
- secretive

END STROKES

Also called finishing strokes, these are the last strokes
the writer makes when making a letter.

What do end strokes reveal?
- the social attitude of the writer
- the speed at which the handwriting sample was made
- how the writer adapts to his or her environment
- the current behavior of the writer
- the attitudes of the writer based on past experience

How to use this section
Provided here are some examples of end strokes
and the possible character traits associated with
each. Because of the wide variety of writing styles, it
is impossible to show all types of end stroke. The
letter "**e**" is believed to be of special importance, and
examples of lowercase letter "**e**" end strokes are
provided at the end of this section. Try to find those
examples that most closely match your handwriting
samples and compare the suggested character traits
with what you have already discovered about your
writer. See also the section on starting strokes.

---

*For more information on the end strokes of the
lowercase letters "**f**", "**g**", "**p**", "**q**" and y see the
section on loops.

Long end strokes

These are symbolic of someone who is a hanger-on, someone who cannot finish things and who is self-protective but also genuine, generous, and outgoing.

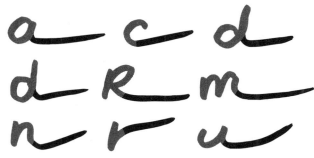

Long and exaggerated horizontal end strokes

suggest a person who is strong-minded but who is also cautious, possessive, suspicious, and a bit of a worrier.

Upward-pointing end strokes

This person may be an exhibitionist who is mystical or religious or who desires intellectual stimulation.

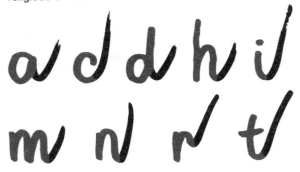

Upward-pointing end strokes that veer to the right

These are indicative of altruism and extroversion and may be used by someone who is cooperative, easy-going, and generous who may have unusual interests.

Upward-tapered end strokes
These might be used by someone who gives
reluctantly, or who expects to have favors returned.

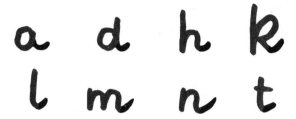

Tick-like end strokes are seen in the writing of people
who are quick thinkers but who keep others at a
distance. If angular, they imply aggression and may be
used by someone who is irritable, impatient, nervous,
or tense.

Hooked end strokes
These imply deceitfulness.

Looped end strokes are used by people who are
poetical and imaginative.

End strokes which end abruptly may be interpreted in a variety of ways. They may be used by someone who is abrupt, compulsive, inconsiderate, reticent, reserved, selfish, and unobliging, but who is also discriminating, honest, self-disciplined, and shy.

$$a \quad d \quad h \quad k$$

$$m \quad n \quad u$$

Unfinished end strokes suggest a person who is concealing and selfish, someone who procrastinates and doesn't finish projects.

$$a b d h k m n$$

Backward-curving end strokes
These indicate someone who is defensive, introverted, secretive, and self-protecting. They suggest insecurity and even guilt.

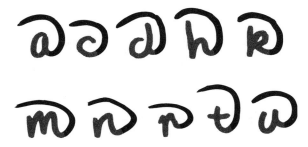

End strokes that curve back to the last letter imply egotism.

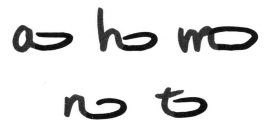

Thick, descending end strokes might be used by a writer who is argumentative, brutal, cruel, defensive, dogmatic, and opinionated.

End strokes which are club-like reveal a writer who uses stronger pressure at times, and this is indicative of aggression, brusqueness and cruelty, someone who might be emotional, firm, and even hot-tempered.

End strokes which trail off are an indication that the
writer may be tired or weak.

End strokes that are hooked to the left suggest a
grasping, greedy nature.

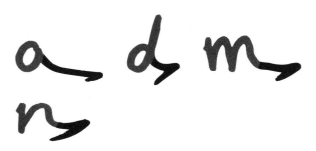

End strokes which are turned left and under reveal a writer who is hot-tempered, selfish, and uncompromising.

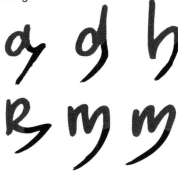

Wrapped-up end strokes might be used by someone who is greedy and egotistical.

END STROKES OF THE LETTER "E"

The end strokes of the lowercase letter "**e**" are considered to have special significance in handwriting analysis.

	End stroke style	Interpretation
	Normal end stroke	Has normal, friendly relationships with others
	Extended end stroke	Generous
	Abrupt end stroke	Ends friendships abruptly
	Rigid, downward-sloping end stroke	Egotistic and dominant
	Long downward-sloping end stroke	Intolerant
	End stroke which trails to the left	Cautious, selfish

	End stroke style	Interpretation
	Rising end stroke	A dreamer, perhaps with an interest in the occult
	End stroke curves back on itself	Protective
	Large hook on end stroke	Tenacious
	Small hook on end stroke	Stubborn
	Filled-in end stroke	Sensual
	Like a Greek letter	Cultured

ENVELOPES

The way an envelope is addressed indicates certain
character traits, some examples of which are shown
here.

- balanced
- careful
- clear-thinking
- considerate
- organizing ability

MR R. LAWRENCE
60, ANDOVER ST.
LOUISVILLE, KENTUCKY
KY 40202

- a dreamer
- careless
- hasty

MR R. LAWRENCE
60, ANDOVER ST.
LOUISVILLE, KENTUCKY
KY 40202

- pessimistic

MR R. LAWRENCE
60, ANDOVER ST.
LOUISVILLE, KENTUCKY
KY 40202

MR R. LAWRENCE
60, ANDOVER ST.
LOUISVILLE, KENTUCKY
KY 40202

- emotional
- outward-looking
- restless
- unwilling to take initiative

MR R. LAWRENCE
60, ANDOVER ST.
LOUISVILLE, KENTUCKY
KY 40202

- afraid of future
- egocentric
- forbidding
- reserved
- self-reliant
- shy
- unobliging

MR R. LAWRENCE
60, ANDOVER ST.
LOUISVILLE, KENTUCKY
KY 40202

- conflict with authority
- idealistic
- perfectionist
- uninhibited

MR R. LAWRENCE
60, ANDOVER ST.
LOUISVILLE, KENTUCKY
KY 40202

- cautious
- doubtful
- envious
- materialistic
- suspicious

MR R. LAWRENCE
60, ANDOVER ST.
LOUSVILLE, KENTUCKY
KY 40202

- desires freedom
- materialistic
- without illusions

MR R. LAWRENCE
60, ANDOVER ST.
LOUSVILLE, KENTUCKY
KY 40202

- avoids strangers
- cautious
- suspicious

mr R Lawrence
60, andover st
lousville, kentucky
ky 40202

(Illegible address)
- difficulty adapting
- uncomfortable with conventional forms of communication

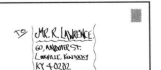

TO MR. R. LAWRENCE
60, ANDOVER ST.
LOUSVILLE, KENTUCKY
KY 40202

(Stylized)
- masks the writer's real personality

On the following pages you will find some real
envelope examples. Test your understanding of this
stage of the analysis by comparing them to the
examples given on the first three pages of this section.

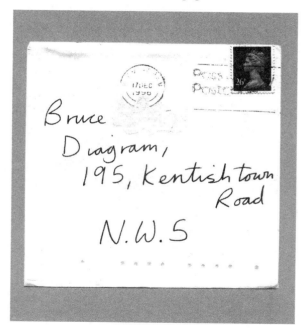

BRUCE
c/o DIAGRAM
295 KENTISH TOWN RD
LONDON NW5

Diagram
195 Kentish Town Road
London NW5

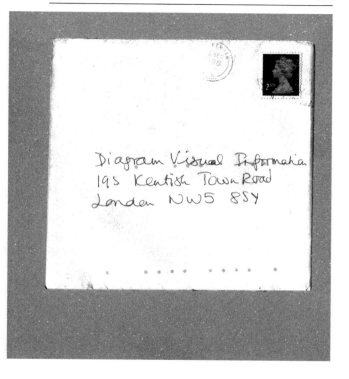

INK COLOR

In addition to the style of a person's writing, it is
important that graphologists take into account what
color ink has been used. Try to find out what color
people would use if they had a choice.
Blue, black, and blue-black are the most widely used
colors, particularly in formal correspondence. Be
aware that a certain color could have been used for
practical reasons. Red corrections, for example, are
often made to a text because they stand out. So a
teacher or lawyer might be more likely to use such a
color simply out of habit and because he or she has
pens of that color at hand.

INK COLOR	POSSIBLE TRAITS
Black	• ambitious • conventionally-minded • efficient • needs to impress
Blue	• friendly attitude • inspired • loyal • outward-going • sincere • spiritually minded • understanding • warm

INK COLOR	POSSIBLE TRAITS
Blue-black	• ambitious • conventionally-minded • needs to impress • efficiency
Royal blue	• warm • sympathetic • even-tempered
Brown	• needs to be noticed
Green	• adaptable • intelligent • needs to appear different • versatile
Red	• exaggerated ego • needs to be the center of attention • sensual
Violet	• fussy • needs to show off

LEFT-HANDED WRITING

What is handedness?
A person's preference to use one hand instead of the
other denotes their handedness. Most people are right-
handed, but a significant minority are left-handed.
Handedness does not just refer to which hand a person
writes with but encompasses the whole range of tasks
performed with the hands. This preference can be
spotted in babies as young as 28 weeks.

Sinistrality and dextrality
- If a person always uses their left hand, they are called
  a sinistral, and the trait is described as sinistrality.
- If a person always uses their right hand, they are
  called a dextral, and the trait is described as dextrality
Few people are completely sinistral or dextral in tasks
other than handwriting. Up to the age of seven, children
can swap from being left to right handed.

a sinistral   **a dextral**

Ambidexterity

An even smaller number of people than are
left-handed are ambidextrous, meaning that they can
use either hand with equal ease. Some ambidexters use
different hands for different tasks; others use either
hand for any task.

Ambidexterity is a trait that can be learned, but the
amount of time and effort needed to make yourself
truly ambidextrous makes this an impossible task for
any but the most dedicated of musicians. Even then, the
use of the preferred hand could still be spotted in a
sample of handwriting from each hand. This is because
handwriting requires the use of such fine motor skills
that even slight discrepancies in ability are noticeable.

The famous Italian scientist, artist, and inventor
Leonardo da Vinci was a true ambidexter. He
wrote his journals in mirror writing, which is
written from right to left, and its reflection can be read
in a mirror. Many left handers find mirror writing
comes easily to them.

How do we get handedness?

It is not known why people favor one hand over the other. Humans are the only animals known to prefer the use of one appendage over another. There are various theories that attempt to explain handedness, but none has yet been proven beyond doubt.

- Some scientists think that it is a preference that is learned, and that cultural reservations about left-handedness make right-handedness the dominant preference.

- Other scientists think that it might be genetic (inherited from our parents). But, if handedness is genetic, then how do genetically identical twins often develop opposite handedness (one will be right-handed and the other left-handed)?

Handedness and hemispheres

The secret to handedness could lie in our control centers in the brain. The human brain is divided into two lobes called hemispheres. Each half deals with different thought processes.

Both sides are involved in thought processes and motor control of the whole body, but the left-hand hemisphere mostly controls the right-hand side of the body and vice versa.

The diagram on the opposite page shows what each hemisphere of the brain is thought to control.

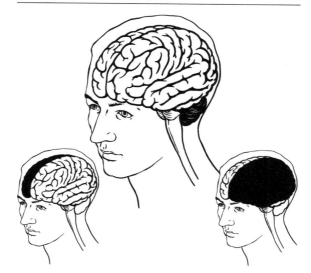

Right hemisphere controls:
- analytical thought
- left side of the body (mostly)
- logic
- verbal ability
- intellectual capacity
- detailed thinking
- mathematical thought
- linear thought

Left hemisphere controls:
- intuition
- right side of the body (mostly)
- geometric, spatial, nonverbal thinking
- intellectual capacity
- holistic thinking
- mathematical thought
- patterned, map-like thought

Right and left-brained people
That part of the brain that deals with language is
usually located only on one hemisphere, most
frequently the left.

● In the vast majority of right-handed people, the
  language center is on the left hemisphere (**a**).
● In a significant proportion of left-handed people, the
  language center is on the right hemisphere (**b**).
● Some left-handed and ambidextrous people have
  language control centers in both hemispheres.

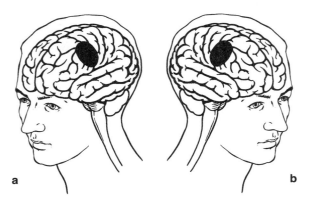

a   **b**

This suggests an imperfect correlation between
handedness and the language center. But perhaps the
link is weak, and can be affected by other factors such
as upbringing, and this is why not all left-handers are
right-hemisphere dominant for speech.

Does handedness matter?

The natural way for a left-handed person to write would be mirror writing; but this would obviously be not a very good way of communicating. So, handwriting can sometimes be more difficult for left-handed people to master.

To demonstrate this, try drawing the two squiggles below—first with the right hand and then with the left hand. Start at the dot each time.

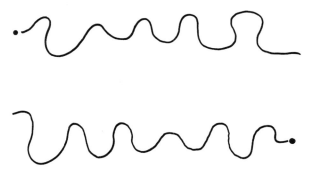

Whether left- or right-handed, you should have found that is much easier to "write" from left to right with the right hand, but easier to write from right to left with the left hand.

From a physiological point of view, which hand a person uses to write with matters little. Socially and culturally in most countries today, little heed is paid to the myth that left-handed people are less intelligent, and the situation is improving. However, there are still many negative cultural associations with "left" and positive associations with "right" that a bias probably still exists in favor of right-handed people.

Being made to write with the "wrong" hand can have repercussions however. In the near past, teachers often encouraged, scolded, or otherwise forced children to write with their right hand, seeing the use of the left hand as a bad habit. Naturally left-handed people schooled out of the habit can develop the handwriting equivalent of a stutter. Such enforced changes can also cause great anxiety and stress.

Some famous left-handers include:

- George Bush, U.S. President (1988–1992)
- Ross Perot, Billionaire businessman and U.S. presidential candidate (1992)
- Bill Clinton, U.S. President (1992–2000)

George Bush's signature

Graphology and handedness
From a graphologist's point of view, however, left-handedness matters because it is important to know what is causing certain traits to appear in a sample. This prevents the graphologist misreading signs in the sample, giving an incorrect analysis.

How to identify left-handedness:
It can be difficult to identify whether a person is left or right handed, but if many of the following signs appear, then you can be pretty sure of a left-handed writer:

- reclined, leftward slant
- starting and end strokes might begin or end on left.
- arcade connecting strokes common

- irregular pressure
- crossbar on "t" broader on right, tapers to left (left handers make this stroke from right to left)
- narrow letters

He walked down the road
and stopped at the lights.

LOOPS

Loops in a script appear in all three handwriting zones
and take many different forms. They may be tall and
thin or large and rounded; they might be triangular or
misshapen; sometimes there are no loops at all. The end
strokes used to form the lowercase letters "**g**" and "**y**"
are believed to be particularly revealing concerning the
writer's sexual tendencies.

Examples of upper zone loops

Upper zone

Examples of middle zone loops

Middle zone

Examples of lower zone loops

Lower zone

How to use this section
Compare the loops in your handwriting sample with the examples shown here for lower and upper zone loops. Remember that loops may vary within a sample, so it is important to consider not just a few words but as much of the script as possible. Look for loops which appear consistently and add your findings to what you may have already discovered about the writer's character traits.

LOWER ZONE LOOPS
The lower zone in handwriting analysis reveals the writer's basic biological drives, his or her instincts and desires (including his interest in sex and love), the value he places on material possessions, and how he feels about the past and the lower part of the body.

Triangular loops
People who consistently use triangular loops might be domineering or sexually disappointed.

Pointed loops
These are found in the writing of people with critical,
curious, and probing natures.

Inflated loops
Inflated loops are indicative of writers who are
imaginative, egotistical, or greedy.

Narrow loops suggest lack of emotion.

Long and rounded loops
These are used by people who are sensual and who have a romantic attitude toward love and life.

Eliminating loops altogether suggests a writer who is direct, honest, and practical.

Loops which should go left going right reveal a need for independence.

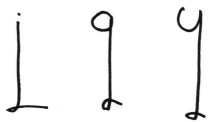

Loops that arc back to left imply irresponsibility.

Flourished loops indicate materialism and ostentatiousn.

Extra-wide loops reveal hypersensitivity.

Extra loops are used by people who are extra-sensitive.

Unusually formed or twisted loops imply guilt or a fear of sexual urges.

UPPER ZONE LOOPS

Remember that the upper zone in handwriting reveals information about the writer's creativity, imagination, and religious aspirations. It is the zone which reveals the superego, the future, and the upper part of the body.

No loops at all are found in the handwriting of people who are straightforward and practical but who lack imagination.

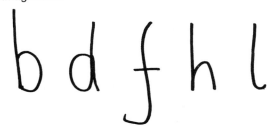

Narrow loops are indicative of writers who are discerning but who may be emotionally depressed.

Large, full loops suggest creativity and a need for fantasy, but are also used by writers who are vain.

Loops wider than they are tall reveal spirituality.

Loops taller than they are wide may be used by people with social aspirations who need to be praised and recognized by others.

Here are some real handwriting examples. What do the upper and lower zone loops of each suggest about the writer? Do you notice that some people will vary their use of loops, always using straight lines for one letter and loops for another, for example, whereas some writers consistently use the same style loop?

Look at these lower zone "**y**" loops.

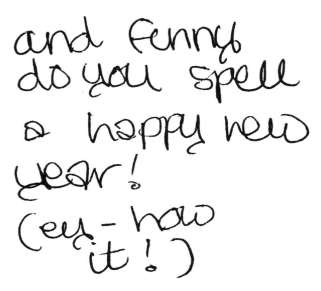

What do these upper zone loops suggest?

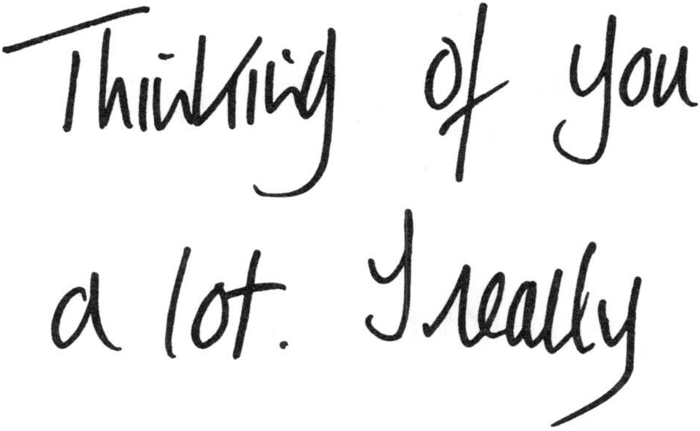

Thinking of you

a lot. I really

How about these?

God bless you all

Can you discern a way in which these two writers differ?

All my love

always,

hope you have a

& that your new y

a new beginning.

In what way are the upper zone loops of these four
writers similar?

all   a   fulfilling

both keeping well:—

this card. I do hope

Wishing you both

Based on a comparison of lower zone loops, which of
these three writers is likely to be the most practical?

Very many
your help.

you for your

posting this
because you
going away.

Although different in style, can you see how the upper
zones of the letter "f" in these two samples are similar?

These words were all taken from the same handwriting sample. They illustrate that both upper and lower zone loops can vary within the same script and why it is therefore necessary to look for consistency in loop styles rather than picking out just one or two letter examples – which might give misleading information. See how the lower loops of the letter "**y**" change in the words "family," "you," and "very." Consider also the formation of the letter "**f**" in the words "family" and "for." Notice that sometimes the upper zone loops are large (as in the "**l**" in "family") and sometimes omitted altogether (as in the "**h**" of the word "the" and the "**b**" in "best."

all the

Very

best for

MARGINS

A margin is the area left blank between the edge of the
handwriting and the paper on which it is written. There
are four margins: the left margin (**a**), the right margin
(**b**), an upper margin (**c**) and a lower margin (**d**). Any of
these margins may be wide or narrow, even or uneven.

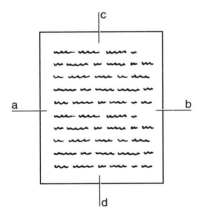

What can margins tell you about the writer?
Handwriting analysts interpret margins differently,
although many agree that:

● the size of a margin indicates the writer's attitude to
  the past or future;
● variations between the left and right and top and
  bottom margins reveal the writer's planning ability.

Some analysts believe the width of a margin reveals
how the writer feels about relationships:
● wide margins imply reserve
● narrow margins imply a need to communicate with
others.

In texts which read left to right across the page, the left
and upper margins represent the past, the right and
lower margins represent the future.

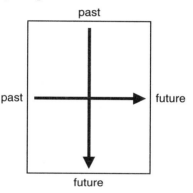

How to use this section
Compare the margins in your sample of handwriting
with the examples shown here. Listed beside each
example are associated character traits. Bear these
in mind when considering other aspects of your
analysis, such as the speed of the writing, pressure
used, and baseline slant.

Making your assessment

When making an assessment of the general use of margins:

- have at least one full page of the writer's handwriting
- have more than one sample if possible
- consider the context of the writing: if what you are assessing is a formal invitation, the writer may have constructed it differently from the way he constructs a casual letter; if you have a small card, the writer may have had to alter his writing to fit the space available.

Questions to ask yourself

- Does the writer use margins?
- Do the margins vary in size—are they wide or narrow?
- Do the margins vary in shape—are they regular or irregular?
- Do the left- and right-hand margins remain constant or do they become wider at the bottom or more narrow?
- Have the margins been filled up with writing?
- Are the margins consistent with the context of the handwriting? Are you examining a formal invitation, for example, or a casual letter?
- Are the character traits you discover from this analysis consistent with other aspects of the handwriting?

MARGIN TYPES

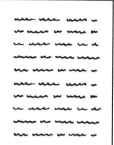

Wide left margin

- cultured
- extroverted
- has high standards
- impractical
- impulsive
- intelligent
- interested in world affairs
- keeps distance from others
- likes lavish living
- puts barrier between self and past
- reserved
- self-respecting
- shy
- snobbish

Narrow left margin

- desires popularity
- desires security
- economical with time
- informal
- introverted
- lacking good taste
- limited education
- limited family background
- mean
- practical
- tactless
- thrifty

Left margin becoming narrower

- depressed
- initially unsociable
- loss of self-confidence and spontaneity over time
- poor planner
- retreats to past and what is familiar
- shy
- thrifty

Left margin becoming wider

- confidence increases over time
- enthusiastic
- hasty
- impatient
- impulsive
- lavish
- needs contact with others
- needs independence
- rapid writer
- spontaneous

Uneven left margin

- does not conform to society's standards
- hostile
- wayward

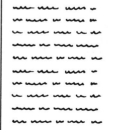

Wide right margin

- apprehensive about the future
- difficulty coping with personal problems
- extravagant
- fastidious
- introverted
- over-sensitive
- practical
- reserved
- self-conscious
- unrealistic
- wasteful

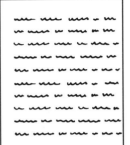

Narrow right margin

- accident prone
- communicative
- gregarious
- hasty
- impulsive
- needs close relationships
- poor planner
- skeptical
- suspicious
- thrifty
- unafraid of the future

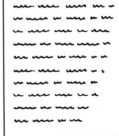

Right margin becoming wider

- fear of others
- self-confidence wanes over time

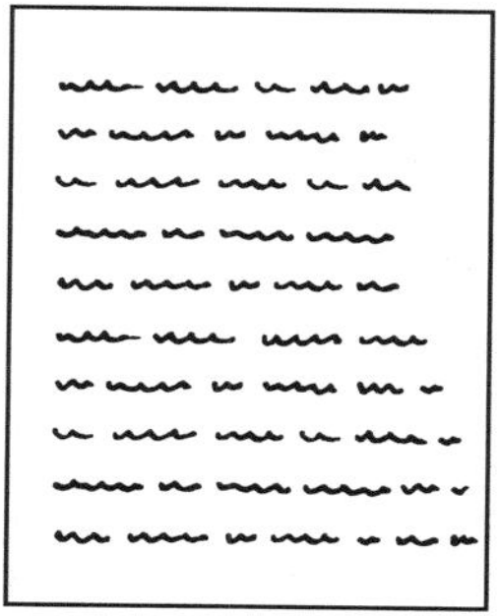

Right margin becoming narrower

● decreasing shyness

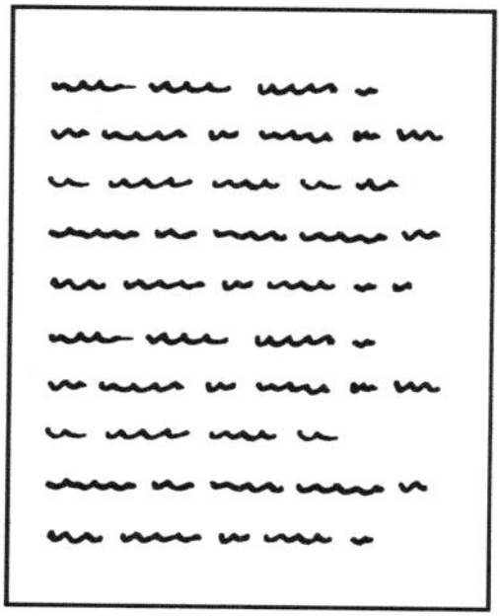

Irregular right margin

● adventurous
● lacks consistency
● likes travel
● thrifty

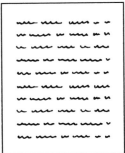

Even margins

- able to size up situations
- business-minded
- concerned with appearances
- consistent behavior
- formal
- well-mannered
- good organizer
- good planner
- tidy

Even left margins: good manners; self-disciplined. Even right margins: anxious, intolerant, rigid, self-conscious.

Irregular margins

- careless
- disorganized
- inattentive
- lacking self-discipline
- poor planner
- unconcerned with formal image
- tolerant
- unconventional
- unreliable
- unstable
- versatile

Very wide margins

- aesthetic
- aloof
- fastidious
- lonely
- needs protecting
- secretive
- snobbish
- socially maladjusted
- spiritually independent
- withdrawn

No margins at all

- charitable
- compulsively busy
- generous
- hospitable
- ignores opinions of others
- impulsive
- kind
- lacks respect for reader
- miserly
- needs to communicate
- poor planner
- restless
- tactless
- thrifty

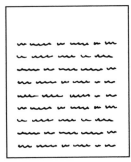

Wide upper margin

- cautious
- formal
- generous
- hesitant
- lacking confidence
- modest
- reserved
- snobbish
- withdrawn

The lower the writing starts on the page, the more respect the writer has for the reader.

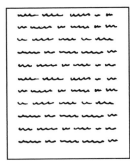

Narrow upper margin

- direct
- dislikes procrastination
- economizes
- informal
- impatient
- may lack education

Feels familiarity toward the reader or lacks respect for the reader.

Wide lower margin

- aloof
- idealistic
- fears emotion
- fears future
- fears sex
- lacks aesthetic awareness
- lacks forethought
- overly concerned with sexual drives
- poor planner
- superficial

Narrow lower margin

- delays the inevitable
- depressed
- eager to express him- or herself
- fatigued
- materialistic
- physically orientated
- poor planner
- sensual

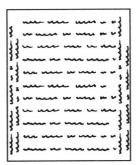

Margins have been used up with writing

- disorganized
- impractical
- lonely
- over-economizes
- poor decision maker
- talkative
- unrealistic

PAGE ENDINGS

Ends with a complete word

- decisive

ends with a complete word.

**Leaves much space at
end of line**

- careless
- neglectful
- spendthrift

end of line.

**Writing becomes
compressed to fit page**

- poor decision maker

writing becomes compressed to fit the page.

NUMERALS

The way in which a person writes numbers can be as
revealing as a written letter. Unsurprisingly, the traits
they reveal often relate to material things and values.

Small, sharp figures
Common among accountants, mathematicians,
executives, and physicists, this way of number
writing suggests concern with financial matters.

Very large figures
Impractical and materialistic

Neat and well-formed
Honest and reliable

Smoothly written
Businesslike and methodical with a practical attitude
toward material things

1 2 3 4 5 6 7 8 9 10

1 2 3 4

1 2 3 4 5 6 7
8 9 10

1 2 3 4 5 6 7 8

Over-stroked
Anxious and uncertain over financial concerns,
perhaps deceitful

Embellished
A daydreamer indifferent to money, or perhaps
vulgar and greedy

Clumsy, with heavy pressure
Materialistic but lacking financial sense

Indistinct
A neurotic or negligent attitude concerning material
values

1 2 3 4 5 6

1 2 3

1 2 4 5

8 0 0 7 2

PAPER

Use of paper	Possible traits
Correct use of unlined paper (**a**)	• independent • a leader
Correct use of lined paper (**b**)	• needs to establish guidelines • someone who feels comfortable with rules.

a

b

Use of paper	Possible traits
Not sticking to a ruled line when using lined paper (**c**)	• has conflict with guidelines
Correct use of paper with vertical rules (**d**)	• needs to establish guidelines • someone who feels comfortable with rules.

c

d

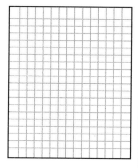

Use of paper	Possible traits
Overwriting a left-hand rule (**e**)	• conflict with conventional rules and regulations
Underwriting a left-hand rule (**f**)	• conflict with conventional rules and regulations

e

f

Type of paper	Possible traits
Large writing on small paper (**g**)	• writer inhibits his or her own self expression
Small writing on large paper (**h**)	• writer inhibits his or her own self expression

g

h

Type of paper	Possible traits
Unusual paper (colored, imprinted, or otherwise decorated) (**i**)	• needs to attract attention • needs to establish identity
light blue paper	• conservative • fussy • opinionated
pastel-colored (especially pink)	• insincere

i

Type of paper	Possible traits
Scented notepaper	• bossy
Child's notepaper being used by an adult (j)	• immature • friendly

j

PRESSURE

Pressure is the amount of force used by the writer when moving his or her pen across the paper.

What pressure reveals
- the writer's personal vitality
- the writer's physical vitality
- the writer's preferences
- the writer's desires
- the writer's degree of determination (revealed by the evenness of pressure)
- the intensity felt by the writer for certain words and phrases.

How to measure pressure
Most graphologists will agree that in order to judge pressure it is necessary to work from an original handwriting sample rather than from a photocopy. Some argue that the sample being analyzed should have been written using ballpoint pen, as this is the easiest writing implement by which to judge pressure; others suggest a fountain pen. However, in reality we all use different types of pen and it is possible to make some judgments based on the type of pen being used (see the box, *opposite*).
When examining a sample for pressure, bear in mind the following points:
- Generally, when someone exerts heavy pressure this produces a darker pen line than when he uses light pressure.

- Pen strokes are said to be "even" when they flow smoothly, without instances of heavier or light pressure.
- Pressure is said to be "consistent" if it remains the same throughout the sample.

Types of pressure

Very light

Handwriting

Light

Handwriting

Medium/Firm

Handwriting

Heavy

Handwriting

Writing implements and their implications for judging pressure

Pencils

Generally, people use lighter pressure than normal when using a pencil, for fear that the pencil's point may break if they press too hard. When using a pencil, the heavier the pressure, the darker the stroke.

Ink pens

Generally, people will use lighter pressure than normal when using a fountain pen, for fear that the nib might become damaged if they press too hard. People who generally use light pressure choose fine nibs (**a**) for their pens, while those using stronger pressure tend to stick to thicker nibs (**b**).

Ballpoint pens

Most people feel confident that when using a ballpoint pen they can exert any kind of pressure without damaging the pen. It is for this reason handwriting samples written with a ballpoint are often easier to judge than samples written using other writing implements. The heavier the pressure used when writing with a ballpoint, the greater the indentations on the back of the writing page will be. The heavier the pressure, the darker the penstroke.

Fibertip pens

People will generally use lighter pressure when using a fibertip pen because they can get a dark, even line with little effort. When light pressure is used, the loops of lowercase letters (such as "f" and "g") often appear open; when heavy pressure is used, these loops may become closed. Heavy pressure also produces a thicker line.

PRESSURE VARIATIONS USING DIFFERENT TYPES OF WRITING IMPLEMENT

pencil	ink pen
Very light	
Handwriting	Handwriting
Light	
Handwriting	Handwriting
Firm	
Handwriting	Handwriting
Heavy	
Handwriting	Handwriting
Very heavy	
Handwriting	Handwriting

ballpoint	fiber tip
Handwriting	Handwriting
Handwriting	Handwriting
Handwriting	Handwriting
Handwriting	Handwriting
Handwriting	Handwriting

How to use this section
Collect some handwriting samples, making sure to use originals and not photocopies. Read through the examples of pressure on the following pages and find those that most closely resemble your sample. Read the suggested character traits and see how they compare with other aspects of your analysis.

Very light pressure
Strokes are fine and some may be barely visible.

Handwriting

- lacking energy
- lacking enthusiasm
- lacking vitality
- lacking willpower
- over-sensitive
- overly timid
- physically weak
- self-effacing
- submissive
- umambitious
- uninvolved

Light pressure

This tends to be fine-lined and, if the writer has used a pencil or ballpoint pen, leaves no indentations on the paper. Although fine, all strokes are generally clear and easy to read. People who prefer to use light pressure when using an ink pen are likely to choose a slightly thinner nib than those who prefer firm pressure.

Handwriting

- adaptable
- agile
- easily offended
- calm
- creative
- feminine
- flexible
- gentle
- ill health
- indifferent
- irritable
- lacking initiative
- lacking resistance
- lacking self-confidence
- lacking vitality
- mentally alert
- modest
- passive
- physically weak
- quick to forgive
- quiet
- retiring
- self-effacing
- sensitive
- spiritually alert
- superficial
- sympathetic
- tender
- tiredness
- touchy
- umambitious
- understanding
- unreliable
- weak-willed

Medium/firm pressure

This tends to be about the actual width of the pen point and is usually clear. Letters appear uniformly dark. If a pencil or ballpoint pen was used, slight indentations will have been made which can be felt when you run your finger on the underside of the page. If written on a pad of paper, a light impression may have been left on the page beneath the sample. People who use firm pressure when using an ink pen tend to use a slightly larger nib than those who prefer light pressure.

- determined
- energetic
- forceful
- physically strong
- powerful
- self-assured

Heavy pressure

Letters appear very dark. If a pencil or ballpoint pen was used, indentations will have been made which can be felt when you run your finger on the underside of the page. If excessively heavy pressure was used, the page may even have been torn in places. If written on a pad of paper, the script can be read from an impression left on the page beneath the sample. There may also be impressions on several other pages of the writing pad. Where a fiber-tip pen has been used, the pen strokes will be fairly thick and the loops of some lowercase letters may become filled.

Handwriting

- active
- aggressive
- alert
- assertive
- brutal
- committed
- conceited
- conscientious
- creative
- determined
- domineering
- dynamic
- emotionally strong
- energetic
- enthusiastic
- forceful
- grudge-bearing
- impulsive
- involved
- irritable
- materialistic
- melancholy
- nervous
- obstinate
- pessimistic
- pugnacious
- repressed
- resolute
- self-controlled
- sensuous
- strong libido
- strong-willed
- stubborn
- tenacious
- vain

Heavy pressure with extreme right tilt
- prone to emotional outbursts

Handwriting

Heavy pressure with closely spaced words
- writer is burning him- or herself out

Writer is burning themselves out

Very heavy pressure

Very heavy pressure

- angry
- brutal
- ill-health
- poorly channeled
  energy

- secretive
- vain
- vicious

Very heavy pressure with slow writing

Very heavy with slow writing

- depression
- frustration
- inhibition
- lacking self-control
- suppressed energy

Variable pressure
Pressure either starts dark and becomes light, or starts light and becomes dark within the handwriting sample, or individual word. Or, certain parts of words and letters (such as the t-bar) are heavier than others.

- angry
- confused
- emotional problems
- frustrated
- lacking energy
- lacking self-esteem
- nervous
- quick-tempered
- resentful
- stressed
- unhappy
- worried

Rhythmic changing pressure

- artistic
- perceptive
- unrestrained
- warm

Unrhythmic changing pressure

- lacking self-discipline
- maladjusted
- undependable

Starts dark, becomes lighter

- inability to maintain
  drive
- tires easily

Handwriting becomes

Starts light, gets heavier

- greater energy in the
  darker part of the writing
- potential for loss of self-
  control

- writer becoming angry
  or excited

Handwriting becomes

UP- AND DOWNSTROKES
"Normal" stroke pressure

For writing to be "normal," the downstrokes (**a**) are generally slightly heavier than the upstrokes (**b**).

Pasty writing

This refers to writing that has up- and downstrokes of uniform thickness.

- artistic
- down-to-earth
- self-indulgent
- sensitive to color
- warm

Thick, pasty writing

$\mathcal{b}\ \mathcal{m}\ \mathcal{g}\ \mathcal{h}\ \mathcal{k}\ \mathcal{l}$

- brutal
- crude
- easygoing
- lacks discipline
- lacks spirituality
- sensuous

- strong sexual urges
- susceptible to temptation

Heavier pressure on downstrokes
- self-determined

$\mathcal{b}\ \mathcal{g}\ \mathcal{h}\ \mathcal{k}\ \mathcal{l}\ \mathcal{l}\ \mathcal{m}$

Heavier pressure on upstrokes
- lacks inner strength
- lacks conviction

Pressure absent on left-descending upper zone stroke
- fears the past

Pressure absent on right ascending upstroke
- fears the future

SIGNATURES

What do signatures reveal?

Your name represents your self, your identity, that part of yourself you want the world to see, and therefore represents your public self-image—what you would like others to think of you, what you *think* others think of you, how you behave in public and what you think of yourself in public.

How are signatures analysed

Graphologists compare the way you write your signature (your public self-image) with the way you write the rest of your letter (your private self-image). It is therefore essential to have both the signature and a sample of the author's handwriting in order to make an analysis.

Things to consider

When making your analysis consider:

- The size of the signature compared to the size of the script
- Whether the script and signature are legible
- The slant of both the signature and script
- How the signature has been positioned on the page
- The pressure used to write the signature
- The style of the signature

SIZE COMPARISONS
Signature much larger than rest of writing

*the last couple of years. Hope both
of you are doing well.*

- attention-seeking
- bossy
- exaggerated ego
- flamboyant
- pretentious
- self-important
- over-compensates for
  being introspective
- thoughtless

Signature slightly larger than rest of writing

*explain why I've fallen out of touch
the last couple of years. Hope both
of you are doing well.*

- ambitious
- proud
- self-confident

Signature slightly smaller than rest of writing

explain why i've fallen out of touch
the last couple of years. Hope both
of you are doing well.

Dave

- insecure
- introverted
- reserved
- shy

Signature much smaller than rest of text

explain why i've fallen out of touch
the last couple of years. Hope both
of you are doing well.

James Weber.

- attention seeking
- inferiority complex
- lacking self-worth
- modest

Signature same size as rest of script

*explain why I've fallen out of touch
the last couple of years. Hope both
of you are doing well.*

Bob

- doesn't put on false airs
  and graces
- behaves the same in
  public as in private

LEGIBILITY
Legible signature

Tom White

- communicative
- considerate
- practical
- reliable

- sincere

Signature illegible

● lacking self-worth

Signature illegible in a business letter

:er you a very high level of support in terms of using the
ng the most out of it and we are continually looking at ways
levels of service.

:o offer you a 30 day account facility to make ordering from

⁄ou on Monday 9/8/99, but if you need any information in the
do not hesitate to contact me

Yours sincerely

● self-important

Legible writing with an illegible signature

> So we will therefore wait
> until further notice.
>
> Best,

Someone who wishes to communicate their thoughts but not who they are.

- creative
- impatient
- secretive

Illegible script with a legible signature
Uncommon.

This reveals that the writer is not interested in communicating his or her thoughts but wants you to know who he or she is. It is a sign of supreme egotism and immaturity

Illegible writing with an illegible signature

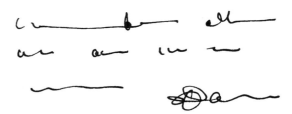

An impractical letter that reveals nothing about the writer's thought or who he or she is. Representative of extreme unhappiness and someone who is dysfunctional.

USE OF LINES
Signature underlined once

- confident
- firm

Signature underlined more than once

Kevin

Patrick Stevens

● needs to be noticed

Signature underlined with wavy line

Marie

● likes to create effect

Signature overscored

- defensive
- egotistical
- insecure with public
  self-image

Line crosses through all or part of the signature

- personally dissatisfied
- rebellious
- self-destructive
- unhappy

Part of signature encircled or enclosed by the first letter

- anxious
- defensive
- protective

- suspicious
- withdrawn

Signature with a vertical line at the end

- cautious
- defensive

SLANT COMPARISONS
Signature slopes to the right

- communicative
- elated
- forward looking
- friendly
- optimistic
- outgoing

- positive self-image

The writer's mental energy is concentrated on his or her public self-image.

Signature sloping to the left

- depressed
- fatigued
- influenced by the past
- negative self-image

- pessimistic
- reserved
- shy

Drooping first name

- writer experiencing depression or disillusionment with themselves

---

Drooping last name

- writer experiencing depression or disillusionment with their family, business dealings, father or public self-image.

Vertical signature with rightward-slanting text

Have a good rest over christmas, we deserve it after stressful PVP lessons!

Robin

| In public this person is aloof, cool, diplomatic, difficult to know, distant | but in private they have a much warmer personality. |

Rightward slanting signature with vertical writing

P.S. and thankyou very much for the wonderful Flowers.

Belinda

| In public this person is expressive, jovial and warm but in private is | more reserved. |

PRESSURE
Heavy pressure on signature

Christine Jones

● energetic

Light pressure on signature

Christine Jones

● sensitive

POSITIONING
Signature in middle of page

● well-balanced

Signature placed to the right of the page

● desire to go forward

Signature placed on the left of the page

- disappointed
- escapist
- lacking self-confidence
- needs security

STYLE COMPARISONS
Style of signature completely different to style of handwriting

- a liar

Unadorned signature

Allan Fox

- clear thinker
- independent
- well-balanced

Angular signature

Graham

Am.

- aggressive

Rounded signature

- affectionate
- warm-hearted

Snarled

- confused
- dishonest
- secretive

Use of large capitals

- needs for public
  appreciation
- wants to be famous

Extremely large capitals

- narcissistic
- proud

Fragmented

Gerry McGuire

● anxious

Adding a period or comma after the signature

Frank Sayers.

● cautious
● conventional
● distrusting
● pedantic

SOME FAMOUS SIGNATURES

On the following pages are the signatures of some famous people. The accompanying text gives you the main character traits that can be identified by a quick analysis of the handwriting. The results of the analysis will sometimes be predictable, but at other times surprises could be in store!

How to use this section

Just read this section through to get an idea of how to analyze signatures, or ignore the accompanying text and carry out your own signature analyses. Then check your results against the text. This will give you a chance to put to use all that you have learned after reading this book.

What to look for

Assess the writer's use of slant, baselines, and zones. Check whether the signature is legible or not, and of particular interest is how the writer starts and finishes a word.

A warning

Always remember when analyzing handwriting that when and where a person learned to write is very important. For this reason, you would not analyze the handwriting of Mozart and John Wayne in the same way. The signatures of 19th-century North Americans often took the form of a drawing of a small animal. This is a good example of how style is affected by era. The point to remember is that it is how the writer's style differs from the norm that is important.

BEETHOVEN

- Considering the era when he was writing, Beethoven's signature is relatively simple and unadorned. Simplified letter forms are a sign of original, unique, and intelligent thinkers who know their own mind.
- The wavy line underscoring the name suggests a person who likes to create effect and be noticed.
- The full, rounded capital "B" reveals an expressive and communicative character. The arcing starting and ending strokes assert a certain amount of self-importance.

Ludwig van Beethoven (1770–1827) was born in Bonn, Germany, into a musical family. As a composer and musician Beethoven's legacy to music is immense. His life was emotionally fraught, however, and he suffered from deafness.

MARLON BRANDO

- This signature is illegible, which suggests that the writer is secretive, impatient, and perhaps insensitive.
- Illegibility can also indicate low self-esteem, as can the droop as the end of the first name.
- The relatively large upper zone and reduced middle zone suggest the writer is creative and has high ideals but does not value day-to-day ties of family and friends.

Actor Marlon Brando was born in Nebraska in 1924. He is most famous for playing Mafia boss Don Corleone in *The Godfather.* A trained Method actor, Brando is convincing in his roles, many of which are powerful but not particularly sensitive men. In 1972 he refused an Oscar in protest against the treatment of Native Americans by the film industry.

GEORGE BUSH

Sincerly,

George Bush

- This signature verges on the illegible, suggesting secretiveness.
- Otherwise, the signature is average, without overdue emphasis on upper or lower zones, for example. Average is a description often applied to the signatures of powerful people, who feel no need to convince people of their status.
- The fact that the signature is slightly larger than the writing does suggest ambition, pride, and confidence though.
- Interestingly, the writer is actually left-handed but manages to write with a rightward slant. Is there more to this writer than meets the eye?

Born in 1924, George Bush's long political career has involved being both director of the CIA as well as U.S. president from 1988 to 1992.

JAMES CAGNEY

- The downward-pointing vertical stroke on the last "y" denotes a cautious nature.
- The use of large and elaborate capital letters shows a flamboyant nature and someone who likes to be the center of attention.
- The triangular loop on the "g" indicates that he needs to feel financially secure.
- The enrolled capital "C" with the small tick reveals a calculating personality.
- The knotted capital "J" shows the writer's pride in his and his family's achievements.

Born in New York's lower East Side, James Cagney (1899–1986) became a popular film and theater actor in the 1930s and 40s. He continued to work until retiring in 1961.

CHARLIE CHAPLIN

- The signature looks like it was written quickly, and that the writer is impulsive, impatient, and intelligent.
- You can see his quirky sense of humor in the knotted bow tie that is the letter "p" in Chaplin.
- The fact that it is the last name in the signature that is legible and not the first tells you that the writer would like to have been taken more seriously than he was, perhaps seen as more than just a fine comic actor.
- It seems that what you see is what you get with Charlie Chaplin since his writing and signature are matched in size and style.

Chaplin (1889–1977) was born in the slums of London but became one of the worlds' most celebrated comic film actors and directors.

SEAN CONNERY

- The downward-pointing vertical stroke on the last "y" denotes a cautious nature.
- The lack of space between the first and last name suggests that Sean Connery is fully committed to maintaining his public persona of successful actor and movie star.
- The writer's loose, garland writing suggests an easy-going extrovert personality.
- The capital C with the closed loop at the top and the capital S with the almost shut top loop suggests a secretive but sentimental personality.

Edinburgh-born Sean Connery is probably most famous for playing superspy James Bond, 007, from 1962 to 1983. A more recent role was the lead in *Entrapment* (1999).

GARY COOPER

- The exaggeration of the lower zone, to the extent that middle zone letters appear beneath the baseline, is very revealing. These handwriting signs reveal that the writer was overly concerned with sexual matters, and the droop in the last name suggests that the writer was needy and insecure about such matters.
- The wavy line with which Cooper ends also denotes a desire to be noticed though.
- The capital "G" arcing over Gary show us that he is defensive and protective.

Gary Cooper (1901–1961) was born in Montana. His long career as a film actor began in the late 1920s with *The Virginian* and ended with Cooper as sheriff in *High Noon* (1952).

BENJAMIN FRANKLIN

- This neat, legible hand demonstrates the writer's orderly thoughts, and the enlarged upper zone reveals the use of the writer's marked intelligence in the pursuit of learning and high ideals.
- The high dot on the "i" also indicates an orderly but creative, curious, and imaginative thinker.
- The end stroke underlines the name confidently and firmly but in a creative and appealing fashion.
- The ornate capital letters are not particularly revealing as they were commonly used in that era.

Benjamin Franklin (1706–1790) was a famous American statesman, inventor, and writer. His experiments proved that lightning was electricity, he invented the Franklin stove, and was an influential politician.

GOYA

- This signature is original yet the letters are mostly simplified rather than ornate. This reveals a creative, intelligent, and communicative personality.
- The balanced middle and lower zones in the main body of the letter indicate a person at ease with himself physically and sexually.
- The upward slant and exaggeratedly looping end stroke suggest flamboyance, but of a contrived nature.
- The importance of his work to him can be seen in the way that the looping end stroke props up the average looking name.

Goya (1746–1828) was a brilliant and influential Spanish painter who had a passion for depicting reality, from everyday life to the horrors of war.

ERNEST HEMINGWAY

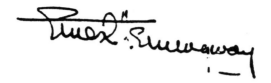

- This fragmented signature reveals the writer's depressed mental state and, in this case, also poor physical health, which can sometimes involve alcohol abuse.
- The way that the crossbar of the "t" deletes the writer's name is a deletion of the self, and reflects a suicidal personality.
- By mixing arcade and garland script, the writer reveals his creativity and intelligence.
- The loop on the "g" going left denotes an independent streak.
- The vertical line at the end signifies caution and defensiveness.

An influential U.S. writer, Hemingway (1899–1961) led a life almost as adventurous as his novels. He was wounded during WWI and committed suicide by shooting himself.

ALFRED HITCHCOCK

- While the writing is illegible, many would still be able to recognize the signature by the doodled self-portrait. This combination suggests that the public face presented by Hitchcock was very different to the private one.
- The rounded lines of the doodle contrast with the jagged, angular script. The writer could have a kind, sensitive side but perhaps also a cold and aggressive side.
- The fact that the face is turned to the left suggests a shy, introverted nature and difficulty in making friends.

London-born film director Alfred Hitchcock (1899–1980) mastered the making of intelligent thrillers, like *Rear Window* (1954), and created a classic horror film in *Psycho* (1960).

ADOLF HITLER

- This signature is angular in the extreme. While it is true that before the 1940s Germans were taught to write in an angular script, this sample has overexaggerated the angularity. The writer is cold, aggressive, domineering, and intolerant.
- The capital "H" is more flowing in style, suggesting that the writer wanted to be liked. Its shape reveals the writer's ability to get away with things.
- The odd dot on the crossbar of the capital "H" and the unusual initial imply a fixation with arcane symbolism, rituals, and secrets.

As German leader, Hitler (1889–1945) brought the world to war and was responsible for the Holocaust, the murder of 6 million Jews.

BUDDY HOLLY

- This open, friendly garland script signature is clear and easy to read. It reveals a creative and sensitive individual. There is enough angularity though to imply that the writer was someone who could use his creative talent productively.

- The letters are simplified rather than ornate, suggesting an original and logical thinker.
- The single, definite underlining says that the writer is firm and confident.
- The writing has a definite rhythm, suggesting musical ability.

U.S. singer and musician Buddy Holly (1936–1959) was at the forefront of rock and roll in the 1950s. Playing guitar with his band the Crickets, his hits included "That'll Be the Day" and "Peggy Sue."

VICTOR HUGO

- Encircling of a signature suggests a need for protection, secrecy, and the avoidance of intimacy. But the breaching of this circle by the end stroke of the capital "V" shows that he can get past these barriers.
- The lack of a surname shows a lack of concern for the social order and political hierarchies.
- The partially connected letters indicate a balance between logic and intuition.

French novelist Victor Hugo (1802–1885) wrote the classics *The Hunchback of Notre Dame* and *Les Miserables*, both of which deal with social injustice. Hugo's life was plagued by tragedy: he blamed himself for his brother's mental illness and stopped writing for 10 years after one of his daughters died young.

MICK JAGGER

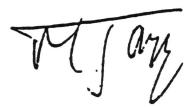

- Disconnected letters can be a sign of pattern-thinking ability, a necessity for a musician.
- The heavy pressure denotes an energetic personality.
- The overscoring of the signature with the top of the capital "J" indicates that the writer is egotistical and maybe even insecure with his public self image. It can also mean that you accentuate your head and upper body in your public image.
- The use of a different form of his name (M. Jagger) rather than how he is better known, could mean that he wants to keep public and private lives separate.

British rock star Mick Jagger (b.1943) is still enjoying an immensely popular career with the Rolling Stones.

BORIS KARLOFF

- This signature is angular but just readable suggesting a capable and efficient personality.
- The rigidity and uprightness of the script suggest some inflexibility and insensitivity though.
- The oddly shaped, down-sweeping terminal double "f" in Karloff shows that the writer is decisive, confident, independent, and practical but uncompromising.
- Combined with the regular pressure, which gives lines of equal width, these signs indicate a certain amount of detachment.

Actor Boris Karloff (1887–1969) will long be remembered for his leading roles in the classic horror films *Frankenstein* (1931) and *The Mummy* (1932). In person, Karloff was a charming Englishman.

JOHN F. KENNEDY

- The writer of this regular, angular script is a assertive and hardworking but the illegibility is a negative sign, indicating insensitivity and self-importance in one so famous.
- The disconnected last letter suggests that this aspect of his nature is kept private and reveals the writer's thoughtful nature.
- Fast, threadlike, and with a rightward slant and heavy pressure, this is the signature of a lady's man.
- The inflated lower loop of the terminal "y" reveals a physical sensuality and erotic nature.

John F. Kennedy (1917–1963) was the president of the United States from 1961 to 1963, when he was assassinated. He is alleged to have had an affair with Marilyn Monroe.

MARTIN LUTHER KING, JR.

- The dominant upper zone and reduced middle zone suggest someone more concerned with high ideals than physical needs.
- Uneven pressure can reveal frustration; perhaps in this case more than frustration with his own personal situation.
- The long lower zones reveal an intimate, sensual side.
- The legible garland script reveals a generous and compassionate nature.
- The understroking of the signature suggests a desire to attract attention.

African-American clergyman Martin Luther King Jr., (1929–1968) led the burgeoning U.S. civil rights movement in the 1960s. He made the famed I Have a Dream speech in 63.

PAUL McCARTNEY

- Embellished with a face, this is the signature of an exhibitionist, though not a particularly pronounced one.
- The unusual arrangement of the c's also reveals a need to show off—as does the doubled underscoring of the signature provided by the face.
- The fact that the face is smiling and simply drawn denotes a direct and basically happy nature.
- The loop on the "P" suggests an argumentative character, and the pointed "M" denotes a critical and enquiring mind.

Born in Liverpool, northern England, Paul McCartney (born 1942) is one of the 20th century's most famous singer–songwriters. McCartney was a member of the legendary Beatles, who stormed the world's pop music scene in the 1960s.

MICHELANGELO

- The mixture of connected and disconnected writing reveals a balance between logic and intuition; this can indicate a successful creative person used to making a living from their gifts.
- The lack of vulgar elaboration and the simplified style of the letters (compared to contemporaries') shows a sense of style and intelligence.
- The shaded strokes indicate an artistic personality.
- Some of the oddly shaped letters could indicate a rebellious nature and/or homosexuality.

Michelangelo (1475–1564), the famed Italian painter and sculptor, was responsible for the painting of the Sistine Chapel and his sculpture *David*.

MARILYN MONROE

- This rounded, curvaceous script with its marked extensions into the lower zone reflect the writer's public image as a sex symbol; an image that was to a certain extent supported by the writer.
- The upper zone is not reduced, however, revealing that the writer also nurtured loftier ambitions.
- There no clear suicidal indicators but the break in the upper loop of the "l" and in the middle of the capital "M" suggest emotional vulnerability and self-hatred.
- The ornately looped capital "M" denotes vainity and ostentation.

Monroe (1926–1962) was the classic screen goddess and sex symbol of the 1950s. The original dumb blonde, Monroe tried but failed to escape her image, and she committed suicide

MOZART

- The generally angular writing style is probably more a result of the influence of the era than a good indicator of the writer's personality.
- Elaboration on the last letter turns the "t" into something that looks like musical stave. Unsurprisingly, this shows a highly creative person with a passion for music. You can see similar shapes at the end of other famous composers' signatures: Joseph Haydn and Franz Schubert, for example.

Wolfgang Amadeus Mozart (1756–1791) was a child prodigy on the violin who grew up to become one of the most celebrated composers ever. He died poor, however, and was buried in a pauper's grave.

NAPOLEON

- Underscoring of the signature once denotes confidence and firmness. This heavy, repeated underlining suggests, however, a need to be noticed and perceived as strong, but is perhaps someone who shelters some insecurity.
- The irregular way in which the letters are joined suggests an erratic personalty.
- The long starting stroke on the initial letter suggests depression and unhappiness.
- The dot to the left of the signature reveals someone still concerned or bitter about the past.

Napoleon Bonaparte (1769–1821) was one of history's most famous and brilliant military figures. He led the French army and seized political power, declaring himself emperor.

RICHARD NIXON

- hook on "x" lower zone like a cross.
- The flamboyant and large initial capital, and the fact that it is larger then the family-name capital, denotes pride in his achievements and a need for power; but perhaps these desires are overpowering the writer just as the letters overwhelm the words.
- This signature is confident and quickly written. It dates from when Nixon's popularity was at its height.
- The sham garland reveals that he is not what he seems though.
- The extended down stroke on the "x" suggests a hot temper, and its crosslike appearance suggests religious leaning.

Disgraced U.S. president Nixon (1913–1994) resigned over Vietnam and the Watergate scandal.

RONALD REAGAN

- This shaky, disjointed writing suggests some physical infirmity or illness.
- The descending baseline on the first name, with its sagging letters, suggests depression and fear or concern for the writer's own personal well-being.
- The inflated capital letters reveal a need for power and attention.
- Large upper loops on the capital letters "R" suggest a friendliness.
- The larger first name reveals pride in his own achievements.

Ronald Reagan (born 1911) was born in Illinois. He was a successful film and television actor before turning to politics, first as governor of California and then as president of the United States. He survived an assassination attempt in 1981.

MARQUIS DE SADE

- The overly large strokes in the lower zone denote a fixation with sex and eroticism.
- The letter "e" would not normally have a lower zone, and the end stroke goes in the opposite direction to which it would normally. These signs indicate perversion and/or a rebellious streak.
- The capital "S" arcs over the name, suggesting a defensive, secretive, and protective person.
- The flamboyant and rounded curves reveal that this is the signature of an exhibitionist.

The life and writings of the Marquis de Sade (1740–1814) inspired the use of the word sadism to describe the enjoyment, mostly sexual, of cruelty. He was found guilty of many sexual crimes and spent time in jail.

FRANK SINATRA

- The flowing rounded capital letters (especially the capital "F," which looks like a simplified treble clef) indicate a creative personality with musical abilities. The flowing script also supports this.
- A high dot on a lower case "i" reveals intelligence.
- The fast, threadlike script indicates that the writer is a ladies man.
- The high crossbar of the "t" denotes ambition combined with capability.
- The inflated upper loop on the k reveals a creative, emotional, and imaginative person.

Frank Sinatra (1915–1999) was born in New Jersey. He had a patchy early career as a singer and actor before becoming immensely popular in the 1950s and 1960s. He continued performing until the 1990s.

JIMMY STEWART

- The combination of arcade and garland writing is a classic sign of creativity and intelligence.
- The crosslike "t" suggests a fatalistic or pessimistic nature.
- The ascending baseline suggests optimism but also perhaps overconfidence in his own abilities.
- The upward sloping, protective bar on the first "t" suggests a cruel and sarcastic nature.
- Consistent pressure shows an even temper.

James Stewart (1908–1997) was born in Pennsylvania. Originally a Broadway actor, Stewart went on to become a celebrated Hollywood film actor in the 1930s, 40s, and 50s. His films include Hitchcock's *Rear Window* and the oft repeated *It's a Wonderful Life*.

BARBRA STREISAND

- This is a signature of unexpected contrasts. Rounded and peaked letters reaching into the upper zone suggest a diverse creative talent.
- The wildly varying baseline suggests a contrary nature and perhaps a certain amount of discomfort with the public image.
- Illegibility suggests an inconsiderate, secretive person, but, in this case, one with a dramatic flair.
- The strangely shaped capital "B" and the reversed direction of the terminal "a" in Barbra point to an independent, rebellious streak.

Barbra Streisand (born 1942) was born in Brooklyn, New York. Her long career has included acting, singing, and directing. She is one of the world's top-selling singers.

GEORGE WASHINGTON

- While many writers wrote with a flourish in Washington's day, he has added loops and swirls mostly in the upper zone—the region associated with learning, creativity, and intelligence.
- Although the upper zone is exaggerated, the middle and lower zones are not reduced, suggesting a balanced individual who, for example, cared as much for his family as his ideals.
- The writing does not differ greatly from the current standard script, suggesting a conservative nature.

George Washington (1732–1799) was the first president of the United States. The son of a successful Virginia family, Washington led the Continental Army during the American Revolution.

JOHN WAYNE

- The absence of space between the first and last name tells us that what you saw was what you got with this man; or that he wanted people to see him as his screen persona.
- The long lower zone suggests sensuality but the triangular loop on the "y" in "Wayne" suggests some conflict with his sexuality..
- The extended loop on the capital "J" reveals a body-conscious individual.
- The drooping last name suggests disillusionment with some aspect of his life.
- Interestingly, the signature is a bit smaller than the rest of the writing: could the writer have been shy?

John Wayne (1907–1979) was a film actor famous for playing tough, macho cowboys in Westerns.

WALT WHITMAN

Walt Whitman

- The signature is much larger than the text, meaning the writer is calling for attention.
- The fact that this signature even has a lower zone (when there is no need of one) suggests a rebellious, independent streak, open sexuality, and can reveal homosexuality.
- On the whole the signature is balanced and legible, showing an ability to communicate ideas and a person in touch with himself.

Walt Whitman (1819–1892) was America's greatest 19th-century poet. He was the author of the classic, groundbreaking text *Leaves of Grass* that explored many previously taboo topics such as sexuality. "O Captain! My Captain!", one of the most famous poems ever, is about the death of Abraham Lincoln.

OSCAR WILDE

- The terminal "e" with its very exaggerated extent into the lower zone (a region it would not normally enter) is indicative of homosexuality. The tick at the end of this descender is a similar sign.
- Partially disconnected letters are a sign of creativity.
- Illegibility indicates a selfish, inconsiderate nature.
- The lack of capital letters reveals a man not in need of puffing himself up seeking attention.

Famous for his biting wit, Oscar Wilde (1854–1900) was a celebrated poet, novelist, and playwright. Born In Ireland, Wilde was a flamboyant character. He spent time in jail for his homosexuality, and wrote the *Ballad of Reading Gaol* while inside. He died soon after his release.

SIZE

This section examines the relevance of the height and width of letters. It is important to consider both these factors in conjunction with the amount of space a writer leaves between lines in a sample of handwriting, as well as the way the writer spaces his words and letters within those lines. (For more information, refer to the sections dealing with these topics.)

What can letter size tell you?
The height and width of letters reveal how a person relates to his environment, whether he or she is introverted or extroverted, as well as his capacity for concentration. The height of letters reveals the kind of lifestyle the writer prefers; the width of letters reveals how much personal space the writer has or needs. In general, the larger the script, the more open the writer is to different interests, ideas, and people; the smaller the script, the more the writer limits his self-expression.

How to use this section
This section is in two parts: the first explains how to measure the height of letters and the second explains how to measure the width of letters. After each explanation there are some examples of letter heights and sizes along with some interpretations of their meanings. Use the information here to analyze your sample handwriting, remembering also to read the sections on line spacing, and word and letter spacing.

THE HEIGHT OF LETTERS
How to measure the height of letters
Letter height can be measured in two ways.

Method 1
Measure the height of lowercase letters across two zones. Measure the heights of the ascenders of the letters "**b**," "**d**," "**h**," "**k**," or "**l**," as well as the descenders of the letters "**g**," "**j**," "**p**," "**q**," and "**y**".

Small
General height of ascenders or descenders is ¼" (6mm) or less: letters are considered small.

Medium
General height of ascenders or descenders is ¼"-⅜" (6mm-9mm): letters are considered medium.

Large
General height of ascenders or descenders is greater than ⅜" (9mm): letters are considered large.

Method 2

Measure the height of middle zone letters, i.e., the letters "a," "c," "e," "i," "m," "n," "o," "r," "s," "t," "u," "v" and "w."

Overall height of middle zone letters is less than 1/16" (1.5mm): letters are considered small.	*height*	] 1/16"
Overall height of middle zone letters is 1/4"-3/8" (1.5-2.5mm): letters are considered medium.	*height*	] 1/4"-3/8"
Overall height of middle zone letters is just under 1/8" - about 3/16" (2.5-4mm): letters are considered large.	*height*	] 1/8"-3/8"

Note: These methods give different parameters for small and medium letters. It does not matter which method you choose to use, providing you are consistent in your analysis.

Comparing methods 1 and 2

Measuring ascenders
and descenders

Measuring middle
zone letters

Small

Medium

Large

Overly large letter height

I don't know whet have started work ew and I really but needs must most of my weeke

- arrogant
- demands to be seen and heard
- egotistical
- exaggerated self-confidence
- exhibitionist
- hyperactive
- inability to concentrate
- insecure
- obsessive tendencies
- over-enthusiastic
- restless
- selfish
- unconcerned with small details
- vain
- wayward

Large letter height

Many thanks for y
d and good wishes we
heartily reciprocate

- absent-minded
- ambitious
- arrogant
- attention-seeking
- boastful
- boisterous
- bold
- careless
- ceremonial
- confident
- dislikes small details
- extrovert
- generous
- grandiose
- gregarious
- energetic
- farsighted
- flamboyant
- immodest
- inconsiderate
- lacks tact
- lavish
- likes luxury
- megalomaniac
- needs approval from others
- needs space
- optimistic
- outspoken
- proud
- self-confident
- selfish
- stimulated by change
- subjective
- theatrical
- undisciplined
- unwilling to concentrate
- vain

Medium letter height

Hope you are both we
& enjoying life — I
sorry we haven't be
able to visit recently
and there are no imm
prospects, I'm afraid — w
will building a new
& all the expense that
entails.

- adaptable
- average ability to concentrate
- careful
- conservative
- conscientious
- cooperative
- versatile

Small letter height

> book keep up the good
> I can't write at all now
> been looking through my
> was going to throw it away
> you could do that after y
> read through it all. I've

- accurate
- analytical
- conscientious
- detached
- economical
- hypochondriac
- intolerant
- introverted
- isolated
- lacking self-confidence
- low self-esteem
- melancholic
- meticulous
- modest
- obedient
- observant
- over-scrupulous

- patient
- pedantic
- precise
- realistic
- reserved
- resigned
- resourceful
- shortsighted
- sophisticated
- small-minded
- studious
- submissive
- thoughtful
- thrifty
- tolerant
- uninvolved
- withdrawn

Overly small letter height

I too like to try my hand at g
heaps of junk jewellery of ever
think I must have been a Gypsy
        I believe I mentioned I w
I teach meditation and psychomete.
spiritualist church that I belong to, as
platform, almost all my friends o'
friends think Im quite potty, bu
the slightest, I never force my bel
they ask me, I believe this all t
twenties I had a bad accident and w
minutes, and what I experienced in
my life forever, you must think I
dont think Im that bad, its just that
seem to have changed my life in so

- deep-thinking
- highly introverted
- overly specific
- possibly disturbed
- withdrawn

Varied letter heights

Hi. Pete

We need to get together
sometime, have a chat about
the good old days. Have you
spoken to any of the others rece
I haven't spoken to Matt or
James for at least a year
or more, I just don't seem to
make the time. So I decided we
must organize something.
a party or just a few drinks.

- confused over what the writer wants to be and what he is
- confused over goals and interests
- excitable
- indecisive
- moody
- quick-tempered
- stressed
- uncomfortable
- unpredictable
- vivacious

LETTER WIDTH

The width of letters reveals how much personal space the writer has or needs.

Measuring letter width

When analyzing letter width you only measure middle zone letters. You measure them by comparing the distance between downstrokes (**a**) to the height of the letter (**b**).

If the widths between downstrokes are smaller than the height of the letters, the letters are considered narrow.

If the widths between downstrokes are equal to the height of the letters, the letters are considered medium.

If the widths between downstrokes are greater than the height of the letters, the letters are considered broad.

Narrow letters

- cautious
- conservative
- critical
- disciplined
- distrustful
- economical
- inhibited
- intolerant
- introvert
- passive
- restrained
- reclusive
- self-disciplined
- suspicious
- timid
- unartistic

Very narrow letters

- anxious
- obsessional

Excessively narrow letters

- austere
- emotionally cold
- lacking instinct

Narrow upper zone

- abstract thinker
- analytical
- ascetic
- critical
- sober

dig hay — upper zone

Narrow lower zone

- materialistic
- realistic

dig hay — lower zone

Narrow middle zone

- cold
- lacking generosity

dig hay — middle zone

Broad letters

- artistic
- boastful
- broadminded
- egotistical
- frank
- friendly
- imaginative
- indiscreet
- proud
- self-assured
- self-expressive
- sociable
- spontaneous
- tolerant
- vain

Very broad letters

- extravagant
- imaginative
- impressionable
- impudent
- inconsiderate
- intrusive
- obtrusive

Broad letters with light pressure

- attention-seeking
- careless
- extravagant
- over-sensitive

Broad letters with heavy pressure
- ambitious
- egotistical
- expansive
- imaginative
- independent
- lacking tact
- outspoken
- proud
- unrestrained
- vain

Broad upper loops
- able to visualize
- imaginative
- perceptive

upper zone

Broad lower loops
- daydreamer
- emotional
- materialistic
- over-imaginative

lower zone

**Broad middle
zone**

- cheerful
- sociable
- warm

 middle zone

**Broad with
leftward slant**

- cautious
- cunning
- sociable
- suspicious

SPACING

This section considers three types of spacing apparent in handwriting: line spacing, word spacing, and letter spacing.

- Line spacing refers to the space left between lines of script on a sheet of paper.
- Word spacing refers to the spaces the writer leaves between words within a line of text.
- Letter spacing is the amount of space the writer leaves between letters within words.

What spacing reveals
Spacing reveals the writer's adaptability, sociability, and attitude toward people.

How to use this section
Provided here are examples of the kinds of line, word, and letter spacing commonly found in handwriting samples, together with some suggested character traits. Compare your handwriting samples with the examples shown here and record your findings. Compare the character traits you discover from a writer's use of space with the character traits revealed by other aspects of your analysis.
When analyzing the use of space it is always important to try to find full-page handwriting examples rather than postcards, for example.

LINE SPACING

Even spacing

- clear
- consistent
- maintains integrity
- mature
- systematic
- unadventurous

Narrow spacing

- careful
- conscientious
- emotionally confused
- frugal
- hasty
- imaginative
- impulsive
- lacking reserve
- spontaneous
- thrifty

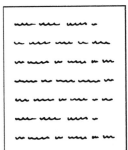

Wide spacing

- ability to reason
- a loner
- broadminded
- generous
- lacking spontaneity
- objective
- open
- self-assured
- well-mannered
- well-organized

Very wide spacing

- divorced from reality
- likes to be alone
- uninvolved

Tangled letters

- confused
- emotional instability
- impulsiveness
- lacks intellectual skill
- lacks reserve
- muddleheaded
- over-involved
- possibly indicative of mental instability
- preoccupied with instincts
- uninhibited

Varied spacing

- erratic behavior
- lacks control
- lacks commitment
- lacks judgment

WORD SPACING

MEASURING WORD SPACING
Some graphologists argue that spacing between words can be measured by the width of a lowercase "a," "e," "m," "n," "o," "u", and "w."

abcde mno uvwx

Normal spacing
"Normal" word spacing is believed to fall somewhere between the width of an "a," "e," "o," or "u," and an "m" or "w."

The eat sat on

Narrow spacing
Word spacing is narrow if it is less than the width of an "n."

The eat sat on

Wide spacing
Word spacing wider than the width of a "w" is considered to be wide.

The   eat   sat

Even
- reasonable
- self-confident
- unadventurous
- well-balanced
- well-organized

Uneven
- oscillates between extreme behaviors
- emotionally insecure
- emotionally unstable
- gullible
- insecure
- spontaneous

Narrow
- emotionally unstable
- extroverted
- fears being alone
- impatient
- impulsive
- insecure
- intolerant
- lacks reserve
- obtrusive
- sociable
- spontaneous
- subjective
- talkative
- thrifty
- weak-willed
- warm

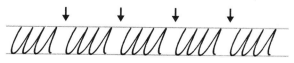

Large
- broadminded
- cautious
- clear-minded
- conceited
- critical
- cultured
- extravagant
- generous
- inhibited
- introverted
- isolated
- lacking self-confidence
- lonely
- objective
- open
- opinionated
- philosophical
- reserved
- self-sufficient
- shy
- socially discriminating

Very large
- apprehensive
- distrustful
- egotistical
- extravagant
- inconsiderate
- isolated
- paranoid
- suspicious

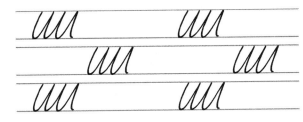

LETTER SPACING

Narrow

- hostile
- inhibited
- narrow-minded
- repressed
- resentful
- scared
- selfish

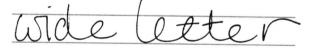

Wide

- extroverted
- socially isolated
- sympathetic
- understanding

WORD AND LETTER COMBINATIONS

Wide spaces between words, narrow spaces between letters

- incapable of intimacy
- paranoid
- socially maladjusted
- uptight

Narrow spaces between both words and letters

- obtrusive
- narrow-minded

SPEED

What do we mean by speed?

In graphology, speed refers to how quicly a writer forms letters and words. You do not have to watch someone writing to know whether they are a fast or slow writer. By just looking at a handwriting sample a graphologist can assess how quickly it was written.

How to assess speed

Look at the check lists given for the three main speeds: slow, average, and fast. To see which type a sample matches, count how many of the traits it features for each speed variety.

What does handwriting speed reveal?

- Speed of the writer's thoughts
- Speeds of the writer's physical reactions
- Depth of the writer's emotional responses
- The writer's intellectual abilities
- The writer's honesty and spontaneity

A warning

Bear in mind, however, that for speed to be revealing you need to know the speed at which writer normally writes. Don't look to speed to reveal anything on a hastily written note executed in a rush. Also consider whether or not physical illness might have affected a person's handwriting speed.

Slow writing
- fewer than 100 letters a minute
- disconnected
- legible
- lower case i's carefully dotted
- lower case t's carefully crossed
- uniform

Have a great time and enjoy yourself!

- attention to detail
- careful
- gullible
- inhibited
- lacks spontaneity
- lazy
- neat
- over-cautious
- passive
- prudent
- reflective
- self-conscious
- semi-literate
- steady
- thoughtful
- thrifty
- wary
- weak-willed

Average writing
- between 100 and 200 letters a minute
- tends to be vertical or almost vertical
- script is connected or partially disconnected
- script tends to be medium to large in size
- legible
- letterforms tend to be more rounded but not excessively so.

The plan is that we will all meet at 10 and then have lunch.

- rational
- realistic
- a good planner
- organized
- appreciative of style
- tolerant
- controlled
- intelligent
- considerate

Fast writing
- more than 200 letters a minute
- writing which leans to the right
- absence of starting strokes
- lower case i's dotted to the right
- lower case t's crossed to the right
- script may be small
- script is connected by garland or thread
- tends to be sloppy
- tends to take up a lot of space
- tends to omit details
- periods and dots are replaced with slashes and dashes

Maybe this letter will help explain why I've fallen out of touch the last couple of years. Hope both of you are doing well.

- adaptable
- aimless
- energetic
- enthusiastic
- excitable
- impatient
- impulsive
- intelligent
- lacks concentration
- neglectful of details
- objective
- pertinent
- poor planner
- rash
- shallow
- spontaneous
- unreliable

Excessively fast writing

- more than 250 letters a minute
- illegible
- extreme rightward slant or angled oddly on paper
- very threadlike
- legible
- faint or irregular heavy pressure
- no embellishments

- zealousness and a tendency to obsess
- lacks any foresight
- in men, can indicate that writer is a "ladies' man"
- rash
- nervous disposition
- foolhardy
- self-important

Speed and size

Fast writing and large size is a particularly revealing trait. Such handwriting indicates extroverts not afraid to make fun of themselves.

Anyway, then she said that she wanted

Variations in speed

If the handwriting indicates the writer changed speed at some point, then it is likely that they are trying to conceal something. Perhaps what they are writing is not true.

We went out for a drink and then went straight home.

Forgery

The only difference between these two signatures is that one was written much more slowly than the other. This can be enough to reveal that it is a carefully (and hence slowly) copied forgery.

STARTING STROKES

Also called beginning strokes or pre-strokes, these are extra penstrokes at the beginning of a word.

What do starting strokes reveal?
- the writer's grasp of new situations
- how the writer prepares him or herself for work (Does he or she dither or get straight down to it?)
- how much importance the writer places on the past
- whether the writer needs to draw attention to him or herself (by, for example, using elaborate or unusual strokes).

How to use this section
Provided here are some examples of starting strokes and the possible character traits associated with each. Because of the wide variety of writing styles it is impossible to show all types of starting stroke. Try to find those examples that most closely match your handwriting samples, and compare the suggested character traits with what you have already discovered about your writer. Capital letter forms have been included here, but remember, they have special significance. More information about capitals can be found in the section on letter forms. See also the section on ending strokes.

---

*For more information on the starting strokes of the lowercase letters "b," "d," "f," "h," "k," and "l," see the section on loops.

Long starting strokes

These indicate a writer who likes to prepare but wastes time before actually knuckling down to do any work. They also suggest someone who is busy, combative, obstinate, and quarrelsome. The longer the starting stroke, the more importance is placed by the writer on the past.

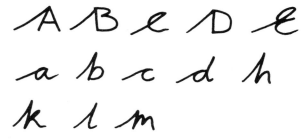

Long and curved starting strokes

Suggest someone who is formal, fussy, and, obedient and who also needs much time to prepare.

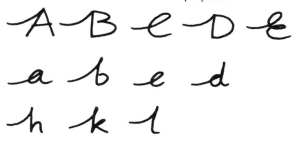

Strokes starting from the lower zone
These indicate someone who is aggressive, ambitious, and argumentative — an impatient busybody who needs to succeed.

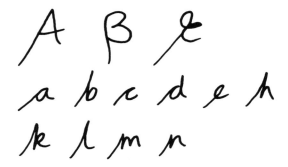

Strokes which begin with a black dot
Often used by writers with deep concerns for the past and by those who enjoy material achievements.

Hooked starting strokes

These suggest someone with an acquisitive, ambitious, and materialistic nature. If used throughout the script, they indicate possessiveness or greed.

A B H L

cm cn ca ch

Claw-like starting strokes

May mean the writer is resentful, obstinate, and money-minded. They may be used by someone who is fussy or has a dry sense of humor. Compare these to the tick-like starting strokes.

b h m n

u

Tick-like starting strokes

These very angular strokes are sometimes used by people who are persistent and who may be hard or quick-tempered. Compare them to the claw-like starting strokes.

A L m n r

Arched starting strokes which cover the letter

Indicate a writer who feels insecure and needs assurances from others. They suggest someone who shields himself in a protective manner.

a c d
g q s

Strokes beginning in the upper zone

Letters which have starting strokes that begin in the
upper zone (when they should begin in the middle
zone) have several interpretations. They suggest
someone who is enterprising, thoughtful, and spiritually
aware but who may also be egotistic and proud.

B C k h h

lowercase "**n**"

Circles in the starting stroke

Indicative of jealousy. Some graphologists suggest that
small circles imply personal jealousy while larger
circles reveal professional jealousy.

m n m n

Absence of starting strokes

Indicative of someone intelligent, objective, and practical who needs little preparation before taking action.

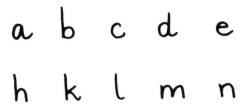

Short starting strokes (which should be longer)

Suggest someone lacking spiritual values.

Curved starting strokes
These may be used by someone good-natured and
with a sense of humor.

Closed loops in starting strokes
Suggest pride.

lowercase "**b**"   lowercase "**h**"   lowercase "**k**"

WORD SLANT

Also called the angle of handwriting, word tilt, or the
angle of script, word slant refers to the direction to
which letters lean. Word slant reveals the degree to
which you communicate your feelings to others; how
much you need to relate to others. A writer's slant can
be a good indication of a person's emotional stability.

Types of slant
There are three types of slant:
a to the right (inclined),
b vertical, and
c to the left (reclined).

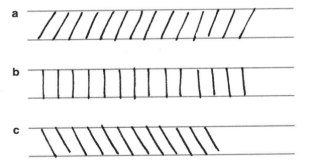

Variations in slant

Most writing will vary from its own norm occasionally. If the slant of writing is consistently varied, however, this can indicate indecisiveness and perhaps even anger. See the sections at the end of this chapter on different types of varying slant and more details about what they can indicate.

Interpreting slant

In general:

- the farther to the right the slant, the more the writer expresses his or her emotions and the more important other people are to him or her; and
- the farther to the left the slant, the less the writer expresses his or her feelings and the more they shut people out of their life.

Word slant does not reveal the extent to which a person experiences emotion, only the degree to which such emotion is expressed to others.

A WARNING

Be aware that some people have been taught to write at a particular slant as children. Evidence of this early influence can often still be seen in the writing of adults, and it should be treated with caution. Of more interest in such cases is how the writer's handwriting differs from what he or she was taught as a child.

Also, as for all other signs in handwriting, word slant should be considered along with other signs.

How to measure slant

At first sight it is not difficult to see whether letters in a sample of handwriting slant to the left or to the right or are vertical. However, for those new to graphology it can be tricky assessing the *degree* of slant. To help you do this, use the slant chart on the opposite page.

How to use this section

1 Copy the slant chart (on the opposite page) on to a piece of tracing paper.
2 Place your traced chart over your sample handwriting and align the baseline on the chart with the baseline of your sample.
3 Some graphologists use both the ascenders (upper zone letter parts) and descenders (lower zone letter parts) to measure slant; others use only the ascenders. Whichever method you choose to adopt it is important that you remain consistent throughout your analysis. Look at the chart to see the extent to which the handwriting slants.
4 Make a note of the slant and turn to the corresponding section on the pages which follow. Note what some graphologists say about each slant interpretation.

Remember, the slant of a person's handwriting will vary according to his or her mood and, because moods change, it is therefore unwise to make judgements based solely on one sample.

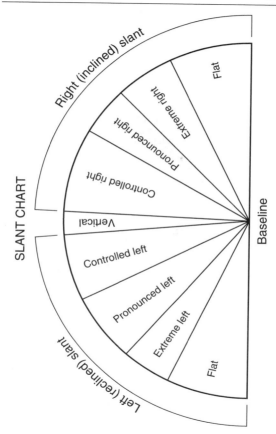

SLANT CHART

Right (inclined) slant

Left (reclined) slant

Baseline

Flat
Extreme right
Pronounced right
Controlled right
Vertical
Controlled left
Pronounced left
Extreme left
Flat

Controlled right slant

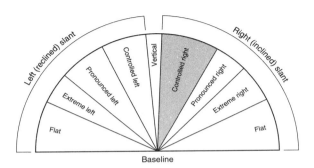

- adaptable
- affectionate
- altruistic
- demonstrative
- dextrous
- enterprising
- enthusiastic
- excitable
- expressive
- extroverted
- friendly
- future-orientated
- empathetic

- impulsive
- kind
- needs to communicate
- needs to give
- needs variety
- moderate expression of feelings

- rational
- relaxed
- self-image not dependent on others
- sentimental
- sociable
- spontaneous
- unoppressive self-control
- unselfish
- uses initiative
- warm

I guess I'll

see you

Have a good

we deserve

Pronounced right slant

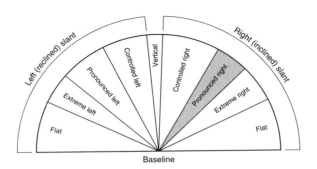

- affectionate
- ardent
- dislikes being alone
- dominated by emotions
- expressive
- friendly
- impulsive
- intense
- interested in others
- involved
- jealous
- judges by feelings not facts
- likes community activity
- needs company of others
- needs praise
- sensitive
- sociable
- sympathetic
- unrestrained

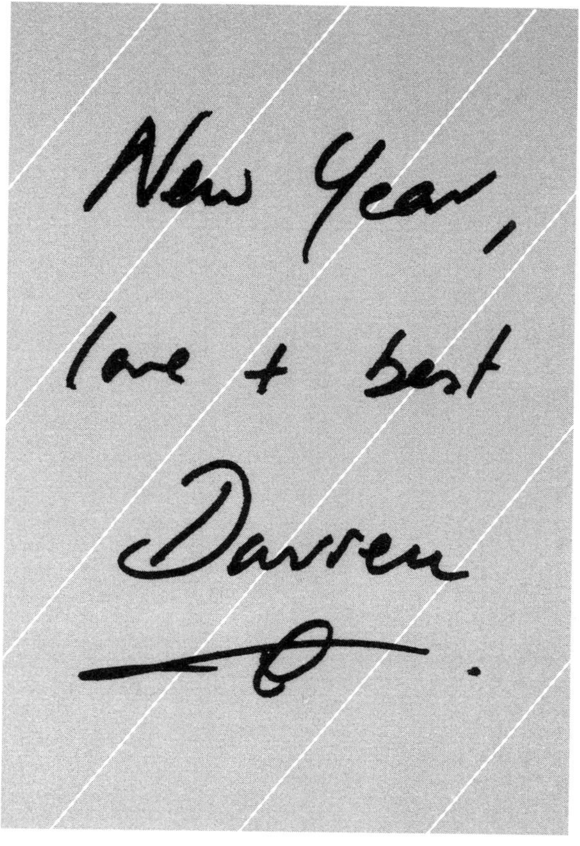

New Year,
love + best

Darren

Extreme right slant

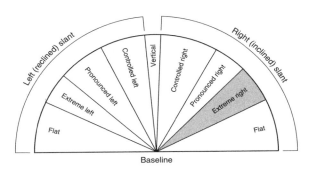

- demonstrative
- dependent on others
- emotional
- excitable
- expressive
- fickle
- hasty
- impatient
- impulsive
- intense
- involved
- irritable
- jealous
- lacks common sense
- lacks discipline
- ego needs supporting
- over-sensitive
- reactionary
- restless
- romantic
- self-conscious
- thoughtless
- touchy
- unpredictable
- unrestrained
- unstable

and all the
year.

love to you

Thank you for
received on the

Flattened right slant

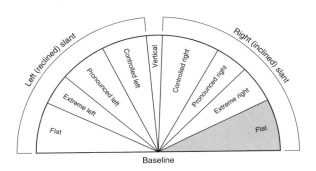

- demanding of others
- erratic
- hysterical
- over-involved
- over-stimulated
- subject to emotional outbursts
- violently jealous

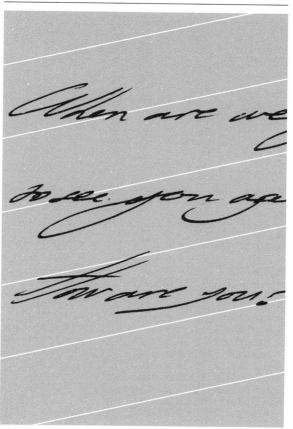

Vertical

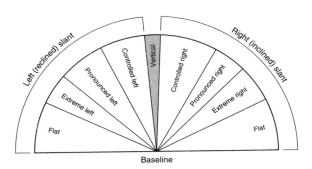

- businesslike
- calm
- cautious
- cold
- curious
- detached
- diplomatic
- egotistic
- emotionally self-controlled
- impartial
- impersonal
- independent
- indifferent
- inhibited
- lacks spontaneity
- self-reliant
- self-sufficient
- suppresses emotional responses
- pessimistic
- poised
- proud
- realistic
- reliable
- resigned
- reticent
- rigid
- sceptical
- secluded
- self-absorbed
- snobbish
- tenacious
- unresponsive
- unsentimental

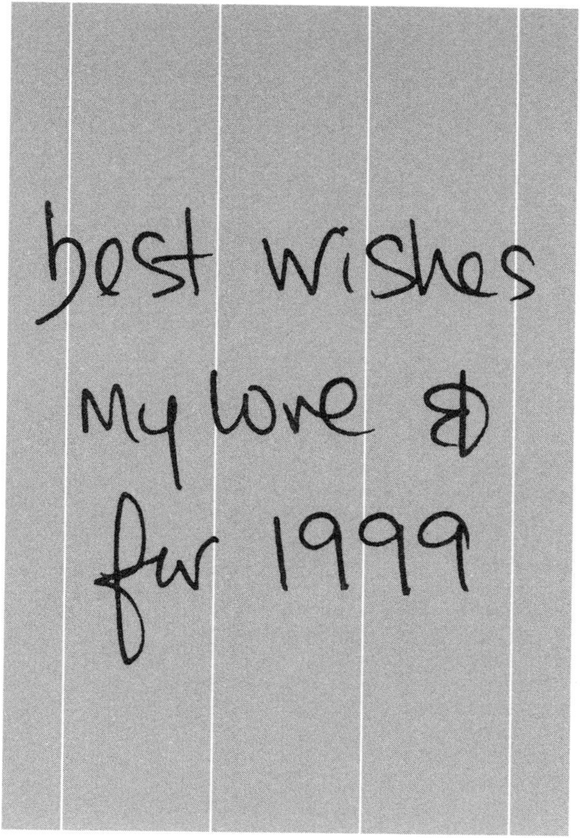

best wishes
my love &
for 1999

Controlled left slant

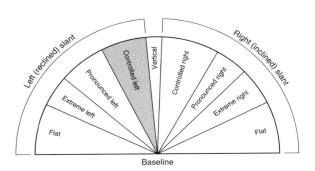

Baseline

- abstracted
- ambitious
- cautious
- conservative
- controlled
- determined
- diffident
- diplomatic
- has difficulty
  trusting people
- independent
- inhibited
- introspective
- introverted
- objective
- cautious
- reflective
- represses
  emotions
- reserved
- reticent
- self-contained
- shy
- unsympathetic

Hope all is going to plan. Wilf has a
virus and couldn't go to nursery toda
so Christmas shopping had to be pospo
We're hoping that he will have recov
by tomorrow for his starring role as a
star! He's a shepherd at school
later in the week but he is not as k
on that, obviously not enough lime l
- as the shepherd has to sit down
the time.

Mam tells me that you are coming n
between Christmas and New Year, :
you're allowed your presents then
we're having Ollie's parents this y
so that Ollie's mum can have a
break from entertaining - She do
know how many pounds of sprou
she'll have to prepare in my ki
I think mam, dad and nana are

Pronounced left slant

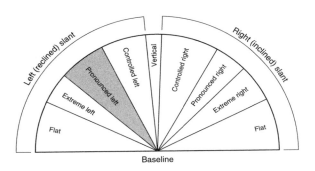

- claustrophobic in crowds
- cold
- defensive
- dislikes socializing
- evades reality
- evasive
- fears the future
- independent
- inhibited
- insecure
- introverted
- represses emotions
- self-absorbed

Dear Chris

Olivia x

With love,

Nick, Kath

Extreme left slant

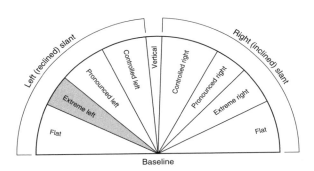

Baseline

- arrogant
- artificial
- conceited
- cynical
- defensive
- defiant
- despondent
- egocentric
- mentally ill
- fears the future
- feels dislikeable
- inhibited
- introspective
- lonely
- narcissistic
- over-sensitive
- past-orientated
- self-conscious
- self-oriented
- suspicious of others
- unable to communicate
- unhappy
- withdrawn

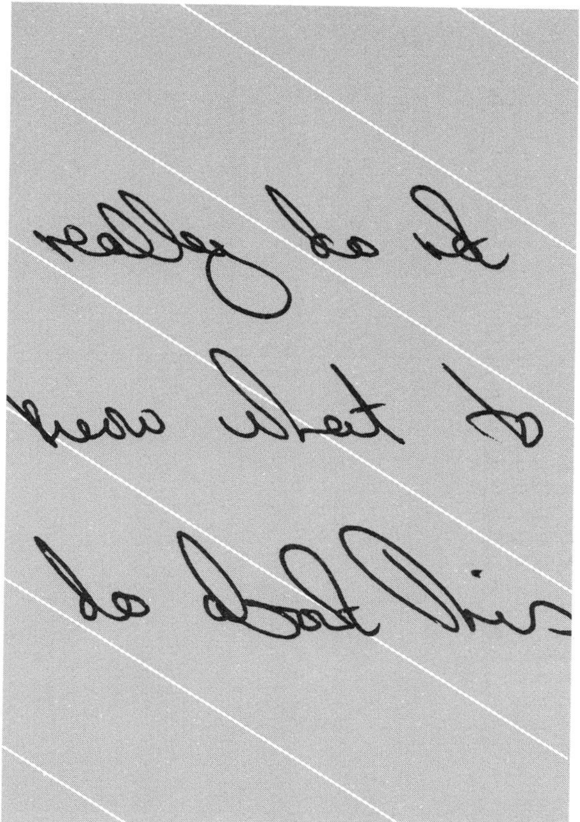

Flattened to the left

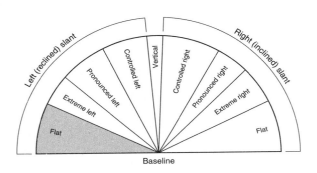

- afraid of life
- afraid of people
- lacking control
- possibly suicidal
- self-critical
- unhappy
- withdrawn

Moderately varied to the right

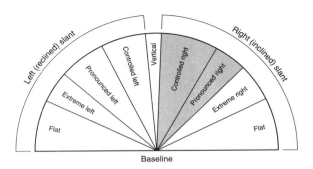

Baseline

The slant of this kind of writing varies between controlled right and pronounced right within the same handwriting sample.

● the writer basically likes other people but is not sure to what degree.

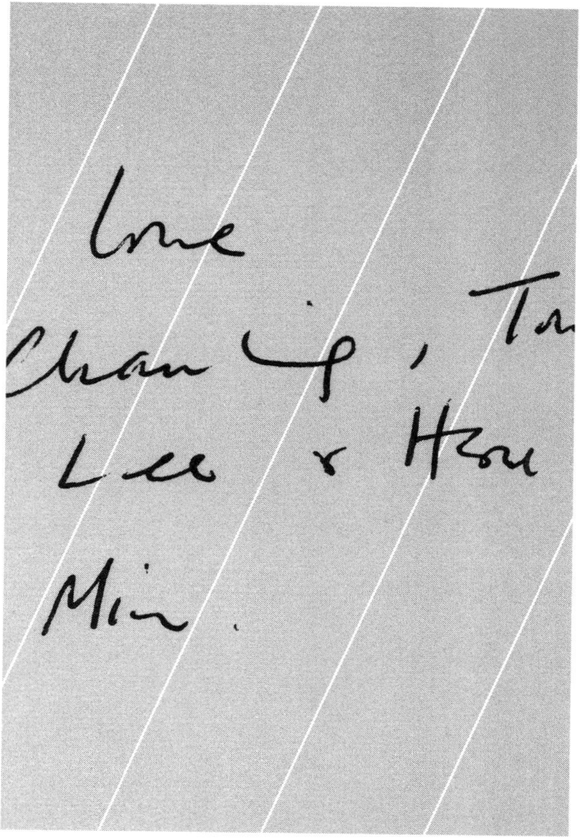

love
Chan ip , Ta
Lee & Hou
Min .

Moderately varied to the left

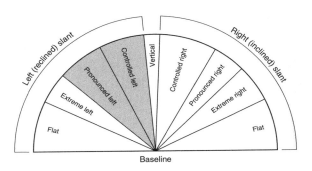

Baseline

The slant of this kind of writing varies between controlled left and pronounced left within the same handwriting sample.

- the writer basically distrusts other people but is not sure to what degree.

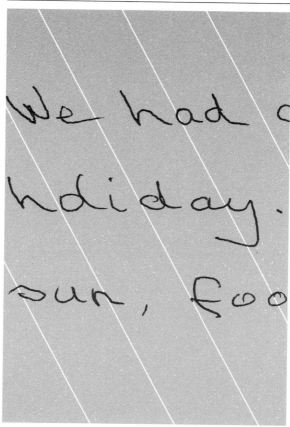

Moderately varied around vertical

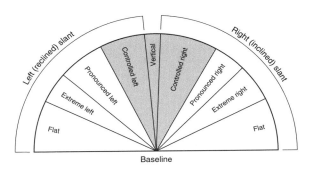

Baseline

The slant of this kind of writing varies between controlled left, vertical and controlled right within the same handwriting sample.

● the writer is trying to maintain self-sufficiency.

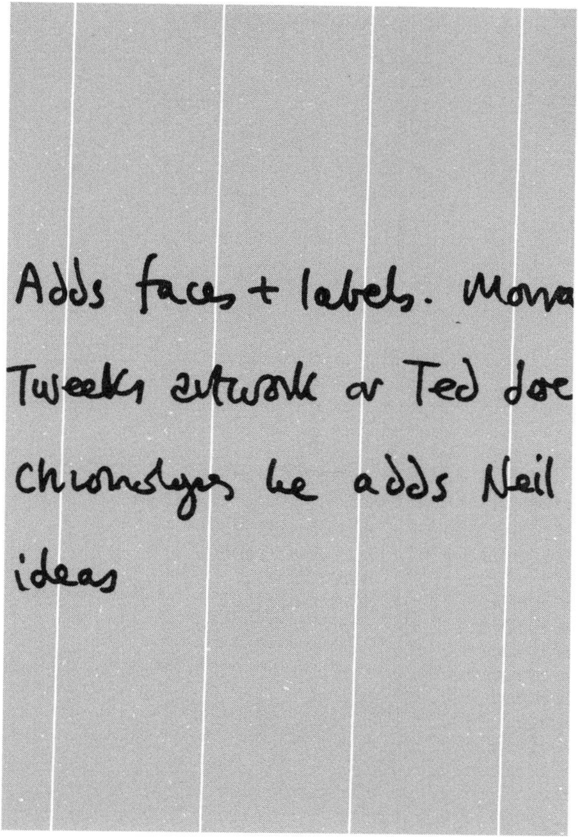

Adds faces + labels. Mova
Tweeks artwork or Ted doe
Chronolyes he adds Neil
ideas

Extreme variation

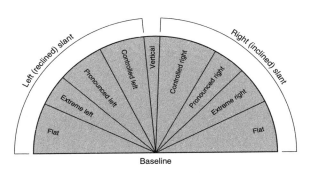

The slant of this kind of writing goes in all direction within the sample handwriting sample.

- ambivalent
- capricious
- confused
- erratic
- excitable
- fickle
- indecisive
- moody
- nervous
- stressed
- undisciplined
- unpredictable
- unstable
- versatile

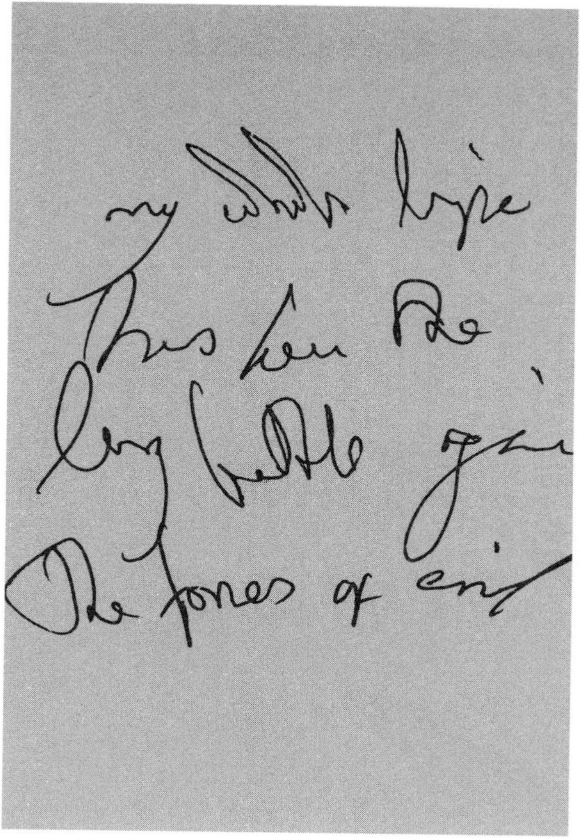

WRITING TOOLS

Although many people use whichever writing tool
happens to be available to them at the time, certain
traits are suggested if a person consistently chooses or
states a preference for a particular tool. (See also the
section on ink color.)

WRITING TOOL	PROS AND CONS
Ballpoint The most common of writing tools, and the tool most suitable for use when writing a sample.	• easy to use • gives a good, clear line • doesn't encourage embellishment or false styles to be adopted
Colored pen	• depends on type of pen used
Crayon	• clumsy • unsuitable for handwriting analysis

POSSIBLE TRAITS SIGNIFIED BY USE

- practical
- keen to get a job done
- not interested in making
  an impression
- unafraid of making mistakes

I am writing This with a ballpoint

- needs to be noticed
- may have underlying insecurities

- immaturity

This was written with a crayon

WRITING TOOL	PROS AND CONS
Fiber pen	• difficult to assess the amount of pressure used by writer
Fountain pen	• needs extra care • encourages embellishment • difficult to assess the amount of pressure used as seemingly heavy strokes could be due to nib shape
Pencil	• fades with time • pressure easy to assess

POSSIBLE TRAITS SIGNIFIED BY USE

- needs to make an impression
- wants to be influential

This was written with a fiber pen

- formality
- has a hidden romantic side
- has a high self-opinion

This was written with a fountain pen

- doesn't like to be seen to make a mistake
- informality
- immaturity

I am writing This with a pencil

ZONES

There are three handwriting zones:

a) The upper zone. This is formed by strokes and loops above the line of writing. Ascenders of the lowercase letters "b," "d," "h," "k," "l," and "t" use the upper zone; the dot of the lowercase "i" sits in the upper zone; the lowercase letter "f" uses this zone.

b) The middle zone. This comprises the main body of the letter as it sits on the line of writing. All letters use the middle zone. The lowercase letters "a," "c," "e," "m," "n," "o," "r," "s," "u," "v," "w," "x," and "z" (when formed small) use only the middle zone; the rounded parts of the letters "b," "d," "g," "p," and "q," and the central parts of the lowercase letters "f," "h," "i," "j," "k," "l," "t," and "y" all use this zone.

c) The lower zone. This is formed by strokes and loops below the line of writing. Descenders of the lowercase letters "g," "j," "p," "q," "y," and "z" (when formed large) use the lower zone; the lowercase letter "f" also uses this zone.

What do zones reveal?

Each zone reveals something different about the writer (see table on pages 000-000). Emphasis on a particular zone reveals a writers needs, goals or fears. Maturity is indicated by the balance between the use of zones.

upper
middle
lower

upper
middle
lower

upper
middle
lower

upper
middle
lower

WHAT ZONES REVEAL

Upper zone
- the superego or conscience
- the future
- the upper body

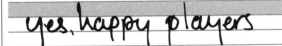

The middle zone
- the ego
- the present
- the middle body

The lower zone
- the id, which includes the libido
- the past
- the lower body

- abstraction
- creativity
- ethical beliefs
- fantasy
- idealism
- ideas
- illusions
- imagination
- meditation

- philosophy
- politics
- religious aspirations
- science
- speculation

- adaptability to everyday life
- how the writer thinks of himself in relation to other people
- rationality
- self-assurance
- sociability

- whether the writer is happy or unhappy

- basic biological drives
- desires
- instincts
- interest in sex and love
- interest in sport and adventure
- longings
- the subconscious world

- the writer's attitude toward home life
- the value the writer places on money and possessions

How to measure zones

Select your handwriting samples.

1 Without using a ruler, draw a line that joins all the ascenders together.

2 Then draw a line that joins the tops of all the middle zone letters (such as "a," "e," "o," and "u").

3 Draw in the baseline rule.

4 Join together the lower parts of all descenders.

Remember that when measuring zones you are comparing the *relative height* of zones to each other and not their actual sizes (in parts of an inch or millimeters).

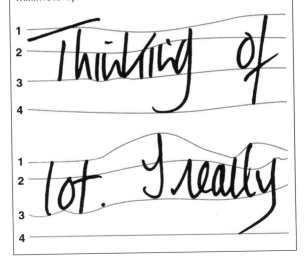

Perfectly balanced zones

Irrespective of the overall size of the writing, a script is said to be perfectly balanced when:

- the middle zone is about half the size of upper and lower zones,
- the upper and lower zones are of equal length.

or

- all three zones are of roughly equal size.

Zone emphasis occurs when one zone is much larger than the others; zone de-emphasis occurs when one zone is much smaller than the others; zone variation occurs when there is a change in size within one zone or there is a change in emphasis between zones, or a combination of these two factors.

How to use this section
Draw the three zones onto your handwriting sample or, preferably, on a photocopy of the sample. Determine whether the zones in your sample are balanced or whether one is dominant. Read through the examples that follow and add your trait findings to what you have already discovered about the handwriting of your subject.

Dominating upper zone

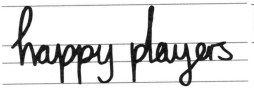

2x size
of other
zones

Dominating middle zone

2x size
of other
zones

Dominating lower zone

2x size
of other
zones

Writing in the upper zone is either taller, fuller, or more elaborate than writing in the middle or lower zones. Intellectual and spiritual development is more important to this writer than the social or physical aspects of his or her life.

- ambitious
- creative
- imaginative
- religious leanings
- theoretically minded
- thoughtful
- unrealistic aspirations
- unrealistic self-image

Writing in the middle zone is either larger, fuller, or more elaborate than writing in the upper or lower zones. Family life is the focus of this kind of writer and social acceptance may be especially important.

- concerned with satisfying biological drives
- enthusiastic
- physically energetic
- practical

Writing in the lower zone is either longer, fuller, or more elaborate than writing in the middle or upper zones. The writer has a primarily physical and sensual nature.

- affectionate
- arrogant
- concerned with appearances
- egotistical
- generous
- high self-esteem
- immature
- interest in social relationships
- insecure
- self-centered
- thoughtless
- vain
- warm

Upper zone missing or weak

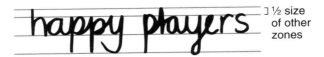

] ½ size
of other
zones

Middle zone missing or weak

] ½ size
of other
zones

Lower zone missing or weak

] ½ size
of other
zones

The writer has little interest in his or her own
intellectual or spiritual development.

- down to earth
- lacks ambition
- lacks imagination
- lacks intellect
- practical

The writer shuns family or social involvement.

- does not express
  emotional needs
- independent
- inferiority complex
- intellectual agility
- lacks feelings
- lacks interest in daily life
- objective
- observant

The writer is disinterested in the physical aspects of
him or herself.

- hesitant
- physical side of life
  relatively unimportant
- sexually inhibited
- timid

Section 3
LETTER FORMS

What are letter forms?
The shape and size of a letter is known as its *form*.
Most of us are taught to form letters at school, copying
from a standard script. Graphologists analyze letter
forms according to the way they differ from such
scripts. Different scripts are used in different countries
and even within the same country. Such scripts are also
changed over time. It is therefore important when
analyzing a sample of handwriting to compare it with
the correct script. The handwriting of a French writer,
for example, should not be graded against a standard
American script but against a standard French script.

a

3

How this section is organized
This section is arranged in five parts.
- STANDARD SCRIPTS provides examples.
- CAPITAL LETTER FORMS illustrates their general meanings.
- LOWERCASE LETTER FORMS describes their general meanings.
- AN A–Z OF LETTER FORMS and their possible interpretations.
- CHARACTER TRAITS enables you to identify those letter forms that may be indicative of a trait.

b

I will be
in Frankfurt
only on
Friday - Saturday
Please suggest a

Two examples of handwriting by people who were taught to write in (a) Czechoslovakia, (b) Italy.

STANDARD SCRIPTS

This section provides examples of some standard
scripts. When analyzing letter forms it is important to
compare your sample of handwriting with the script the
writer was most likely to have used when learning to
write. Remember that different schools use different
scripts and that scripts are often modernized.

This script was introduced in Turkish schools designed
to teach children how to write in the Western style.

Üşüdüm üşüdüm.

Daldan elma düşürdüm.

Elmamı yediler.

Bana cüce dediler.

Cücelikten çıktım.

Ablama gittim.

Ablam pilav pişirmiş.

İçine fare düşürmüş.

Fareyi ne yapmalı.

Minareden atmalı.

Minarede bir kuş var.

Kanadında gümüş var.

Eniştemin cebinde.

Türlü türlü yemiş var

This is the old-style German script.

i   r   n   u   ü

m   l   b   d   qu

p   h   k   i   t   f

o   ö   a   ä   au

äu   ai   c   e   ei

ie   eu   g   v   η   x

w   z   ſ   ſſ   ß   ch

ck sch st sp

O Ö Q U Ü

C G D P R

B I J L E

F T H K X

A Ä N V W

n m s z

Taken from a 1936 German teaching aid, this is an
example of the new-style German script.

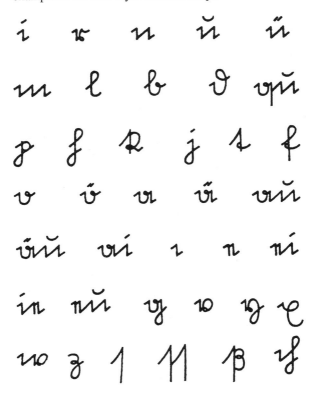

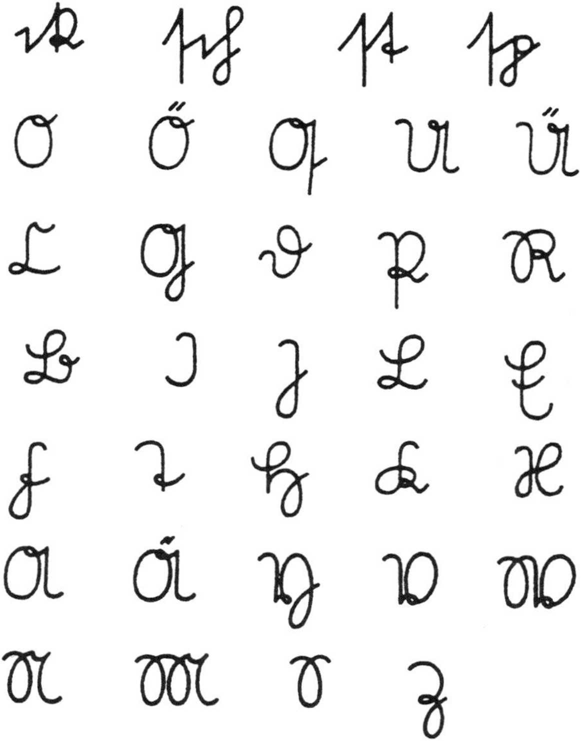

A standard practice letter designed to help German
schoolchildren master the new style German script.

Lieber Emil!

*Weil ich's doch schon so gut kann,
muß ich Dir's einmal schreiben.
Denke Dir, die Hilde ist wieder
da. Du weißt doch, die mit dem
Loch im Kopfe. Über eine Woche
war sie in der Puppenklinik.
Der hat sie immer zu Arzenei
eingekrickt. Onkel Heinrich
weiß das ganz genau. Der ist
sie wieder heil geworden. Sie
saß unter dem Tannenbäume.
Nein, wie ich mich freute!*

Heil Hitler!

Deine beste

Lenchen.

This is an example of a standard English lowercase script.

a b c d e f

g h i j k l

m n o p q

r s t u v

w x y z

This is taken from a 1973 Hong Kong teaching aid designed to help Chinese schoolchildren master the Western-style handwriting script.

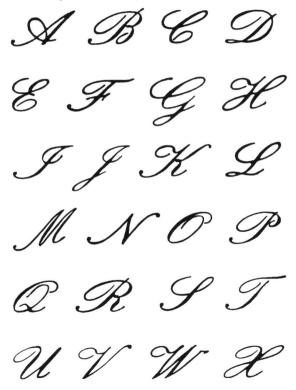

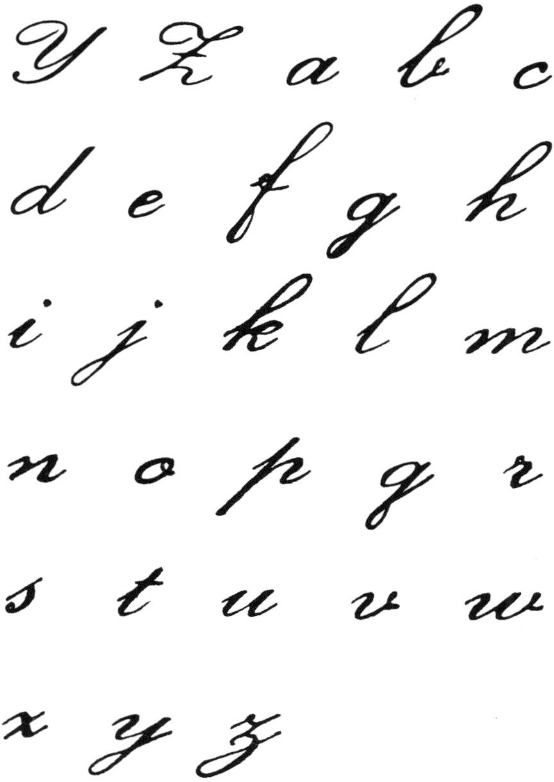

Y Z a b c

d e f g h

i j k l m

n o p q r

s t u v w

x y z

This is a practice letter taken from a Portuguese
teaching aid. Note the formation of capitals.

Ontem fui

Abel e os pais.

ver o farol do

Subimos

passear com o

Gostei muito de

Cabo da Roca.

uma escada para

Below are an alphabet and practice examples from a 1979 Vietnamese handwriting teaching aid. Note the unusual way the lowercase letter "o" is joined to other lowercase letters.

ôm rơm

lợn con _ đun rơm

vải mới _ tai lợn

e ê n m d đ đo da

r q qu quạ củ từ

chữ viết thường **chữ in thường**	h h	q q'
a **a**	i i	r r
b **b**	k k	s s
c **c**	l l	t t
d **d**	m m	u u
đ **đ**	n n	v v
e **e**	o o	x x
g **g**	p p	y y

Note how, in this example of a 1978 Spanish handwriting teaching aid, the lowercase "s" is not joined to other lowercase letters. Note too that, unlike many other script forms, capitals are not linked to lowercase letters.

Adela se va

Ese chico me

Utiliza mi

See also the unusual way the lowercase "z" is formed,
with a crossbar.

de aquí.

conocía.

lápiz.

Compare the way the lowercase "z" is formed in this
example of a standard Rwandan handwriting script with
the way the "z" is formed in other scripts.

walize witukana
iwacu muli peyiza
wali uzi ko igihug
hamagara uwo mu
uwizeye yiga mu

Look at the simplistic way the lowercase letter "t" is
formed in this standard French script.

la grue charge une
auto sur le bateau.

les leçons sont
finies: voici les
vacances!

CAPITAL LETTER FORMS

Characteristics of capital letters
- Capital letters reflect a writer's evaluation of him- or herself—the ego and public face. They are a measure of the writer's confidence in his or her ability.
- They are generally of a different configuration from lowercase letter forms.
- They are generally larger than lowercase letter forms.
- They should dominate the handwriting.
- They are used to identify something that matters—people, places, and things—to begin sentences, and for the pronoun "I."

A B C D E F G
H I J K L M N
O P Q R S T U
V W X Y Z

Measuring capitals

Capitals are measured across the upper and middle zones. They should be twice the size of middle zone formations.

Capitals which are consistent with script size are as tall as lowercase letters with ascenders (**a**) or up to 1¹/₂ times the overall size of the script (**b**).

a

b

How to use this section

This section provides illustrations of the general meanings of certain types of commonly written capitals. For more detailed information about a particular letter form that has been written as a capital, look up the letter in question in the A–Z of letter forms section.

SIZE OF CAPITAL: CHARACTER TRAITS

Consistent with script size
- a confident writer

Slightly larger than script size
- a confident writer

Large in relation to script
- insecurtity expressed as egotism
- ambition
- vanity
- regard for position and status
- a need to be recognized as important
- may like to show off

very exaggerated
- pomposity
- can also be an indication of hallucinations, megalomania, or mental illness

Size varies throughout script
- writer is unable to maintain self-confidence

SIZE OF CAPITAL: CHARACTER TRAITS

Small in relation to script size
- insecurity expressed as a lack of self-confidence
- concentration
- economy
- humility
- inferiority
- intelligence
- love of detail
- modesty
- pettiness
- reserve

SHAPE OF CAPITAL: CHARACTER TRAITS

Narrow

- inhibition
- reserve
- shyness
- thriftiness

Broad

- arrogance
- impertinence
- self-conceit
- vulgarity
- wastefulness

Angular

- cleverness
- criticism
- realism
- resentfulness
- rigidity

STYLE OF CAPITAL: CHARACTER TRAITS

Simplified

- clear thinking
- creativity
- cultural interests
- directness
- intelligence
- maturity
- objectivity
- sincerity
- straightforwardness

Ornate

- artistic tendencies
- bad taste
- concealment
- conceitedness
- showmanship
- ostentation
- vulgarity

Unusual

- eccentricity
- intelligence
- originality

Unconnected

- intuitiveness

STYLE OF CAPITAL: CHARACTER TRAITS

About	**Vertical capitals followed by slanted letters** • cautious but with the ability to overcome inhibitions
taMe	**Use of capitals within a word made of lowercase letters** • a need to be noticed
About	**Style of capitals varies from rest of letters** • creativity • independence • unreliability • versatility
Dear Daves	**Style of capitals varies for the same letter throughout the script** • versatility
dear	**Capitals made to look like lowercase but larger in size** • desire to simplify things • modesty
dear dot	**Elimination of capitals** • need for attention

LOWERCASE LETTER FORMS

The form of lowercase letters reflects a writer's
emotional responses and temperament as well as his
outlook on life.

How to use this section
This section provides illustrations of the general
meanings of certain types of commonly written small
letter forms (which apply *irrespective of the letter
that has been shown*). For more detailed information
about a particular letter form, look up the letter in
question in the A–Z of letter forms section.

MIDDLE ZONE LOOPS

Narrow loops
- caution
- skepticism
- secrecy

Closed loops
- caution
- skepticism
- secrecy

Filled loops
- sensuality

OPEN AND CLOSED OVALS

Ovals with an opening at the top where it should be closed
- gullibility
- openness
- talkativeness

Closed ovals which should be open
- reservation
- secretiveness
- suspiciousness

Closed ovals tied on the right (hidden loops)
- deceitfulness
- secretiveness
- sensitivity

Closed ovals tied on the left (hidden loops)
- rationalization
- difficulty facing self-truths

Small tight loops at the top
- diplomacy

UPPER ZONE LOOPS

Large full loops
- creativity
- fantasist
- vanity

Loops taller than they are wide
- spirituality

Loops wider than they are tall
- social aspirations
- need for praise
- need for recognition

Narrow loops
- discernment
- emotional depression

Elimination of loops
- practicality
- straightforwardness

LOWER ZONE LOOPS

Elimination of loops
- bluntness
- honesty
- directness
- practicality

Narrow loops
- lack of emotion

Long and rounded
- sensual, with a romantic attitude toward love and life

Inflated
- imaginative
- egotistical
- greedy

Pointed loops
- critical
- curious
- probing

Triangular loops
- domineering, sexually disappointed

continued

LOWER ZONE LOOPS (continued)

Unusually formed or twisted return loops
- guilt
- fear of sexual urges

Flourished loops
- ostentatiousness
- love of material things

Extra loops
- sensitivity

Wide extra loops
- hyper-sensitivity

Arc stroke back to left
- irresponsibility

Loops which should go left going right
- need for independence

OTHER SMALL LETTER FORMS

Retracing
- irresolution
- tension

Tall and narrow
- idealism
- religious

Printed
- likes reading

Made like numbers
- Familiarity with numbers

Unusual shapes
- sexual quirkiness

Plain and uncomplicated
- intelligent
- unpretentious

AN A–Z OF LETTER FORMS

This section provides examples of capitals and
lowercase letter forms and their meanings. Certain
letters (whether appearing as capitals or in lowercase)
are believed to provide clues to specific areas of a
writer's personality and behavior:

Letter	Reveals information about the writer's:
A	honesty, openness, and talkativeness
B	communication and expressiveness
C	openness (the more closed the letter, the more closed and into himself is the writer)
D	attire, creativity, self-conduct, sensitivity, and talkativeness
F	organization and planning ability. The lowercase "f" indicates the writer's ability to carry out ideas.
G	attitudes toward sex. Lower zone loops of the small letter "g" indicate the writer's sexual tendencies.
H	spiritual values
I	feelings toward the importance of detail and punctiliousness. Capital "I" reflects the

image the writer has of himself; it may indicate the writer's relationship with his or her parents; it reveals motivation, and provides clues to pride and vanity, modesty or unselfishness. The lowercase "i" reveals the writer's ability to handle details.

K attitudes toward the opposite sex, attitudes toward authority, the extent to which the writer is extrovert or introvert

M communication behavior, the extent of the writer's extroversion or introversion, ego and feelings toward responsibility

N communication behavior, the extent of their extroversion or introversion and feelings toward responsibility

O honesty, openness, and talkativeness

P physical activity

R ability to use the hands, pride and taste for music

T ambition, energy, enthusiasm, and work aspirations. The stronger the crosses on lowercase "t" bars, the stronger the writer.

Y materialism and money. Lower zone loops of the small letter "y" indicate the writer's sexual tendencies.

How to use these tables
Look for the capital or lowercase letter form that most
closely resembles the sample of handwriting you are
attempting to analyze. Read what the letter form
suggests about the character traits of the writer in
question. Never accept a characteristic trait in
isolation—always compare it with other aspects of your
sample analysis, such as the general letter layout,
pressure used, slant of the lines, etc.

CAPITAL A

CROSSBAR
missing crossbar

- careless
- lacking in
  consideration

low crossbar

- subordinate

curved crossbar

- easygoing
- an entertainer

double crossbar

- idiosyncratic

ENDING STROKE
looped at start and end

- vain

low end stroke

- resentful

hooked

- irresponsible
- concerned with past
- self-centered

rolls to left

- egotistic

shorter than starting stroke

- ambitious

"deletes" the letter

- disappointed

SHAPE
square

- interested in construction

plain (medium-sized)

- cultured
- intelligent
- forthright

rounded

- constructive
- someone who makes dreams come true

broad

- generous

narrow

- inhibited
- reserved
- shy

**STARTING STROKE
extended**

- has a strong
  attachment to
  the past

**begins below the line
of the letter**

- ambitious
- quarrelsome
- a busybody

**starts with an arc
to the left**

- avaricious

starts with a black point

- enjoys
  material
  achievements

**starts with a black point
extended to the left**

- trouble in
  past history

starts wiith an angle

- hard

**starts with a
moderate loop**

- paternal
- protective

starts with a reverse loop

- money-minded

knotted

- tough
- thorough

knotted, with a large loop

- persistent
- paternal
- protective
- pride in achievements

STYLE
crossed lines at top

- inexact
- unconventional

three crossed sticks

- sarcastic

open top

- honest
- inaccurate
- open
- talkative

angular with checks

- clever
- realistic
- resentful
- rigid

embellished

- ostentatious
- vulgar

unusually shaped

- tendency to perversion and excess

triangular

- defensive
- dislikes interference

LOWER CASE a

AS CAPITAL A
enlarged small letter

- modest

BODY OF LETTER
closed

- discreet
- diplomatic
- honest
- reserved
- secretive

enrolled

- family-orientated
- secretive

open on left

- egotistic
- greedy
- untrustworthy

made up of several circles

- fixed ideas
- lives in own world

open at top

- honest
- talkative

open at bottom

- dishonest
- hypocritical
- lacks moral values

filled with ink

- jealous
- sensual

SHAPE
narrow

- narrow-minded
- reserved
- secretive

broad

- imaginative

broad and open

- talkative

square

- has mechanical ability

like two semicircles

- tactful

STROKE
covers letter

- misinterprets self

**starts at right of
down stroke**

- egotistic
- fusses

angular end stroke

- greedy
- may be
  resentful

**STYLE
hook inside**

- deceptive

circle inside

- cunning
- dishonest
- evasive
- selfish

knotted on right

- secretive
- may be
  dishonest
  with others

knotted on left

- rationalizes
- may not
  be honest
  with self

double knot

- vain
- dishonest

**narrow knots (on
regular shaped a)**

- tells white lies

amended

- nervous

circled (twice)

- deceives self

CAPITAL B

END STROKE
claw to left

- egotistic
- irresponsible
- concerned with past and self

SHAPE
regular

- intelligent
- literate
- forthright

extends to left

- self-important

full and round

- egotistic
- emotional
- generous

enrolled

- egotistic

narrow

- inhibited
- reserved
- shy

narrow second arc

- cautious

angular

- clever
- realistic
- resentful
- rigid

wide second arc

- gullible

angular in lower zone

- determined to get own way
- resentful

square

- constructive-minded

strange shape

- tendency to perversion

regular and open at bottom

- talkative

STARTING STROKE wide

- a bluffer

reaching

- enterprising
- thoughtful

STYLE
elaborate

- fussy
- ostentatious
- vulgar

like the number 13

13

- familiar with figures

LOWER CASE b

END STROKE
looped

- imaginative
- poetical

SHAPE
tall and narrow

- idealistic
- possibly religious

short and full

b

- humble
- likes to talk about him- or herself

pointed at top

b

- resentful

STARTING STROKE
rounded

- humorous
- talkative

initial check

- persistent

long

- fussy

looped

- proud

circular

- humorous

STYLE
printed

- literary

unfinished

- doesn't finish things

wide upstroke

- expressive
- imaginative

sharp upstroke

- resentful
- uncompromising

amended

- hypo-chondriac
- neurotic
- self-tormenting

enrolled

- egotistic
- greedy

closed upstroke

- has good business sense
- wary

like the number 6

- familiar with figures

hooked

- obstinate

CAPITAL C

**END STROKE
looped**

- money-minded

circular

- egotistic

extended to right

- self-admiring

**SHAPE
regular**

- intelligent
- literate
- plain
- forthright

large

- idealistic
- kind

**enrolled with loops at
top and bottom**

- deceitful
- egotistic

narrow

- inhibited
- reserved
- shy

sharp

- aggressive
- clever
- realistic
- resentful
- rigid

square

- aggressive
- constructive-
  minded

crescentlike

- ambitious
- makes
  dreams
  come true

unusual shape

- tendency to perversion

angular at top and bottom

- resentful
- needs to get his or her own way

STARTING STROKE
upright stroke at top

- direct
- enterprising
- resentful
- sarcastic
- spiritually aware

vertical loop

- feels responsible for others

circular

- concealing
- shrewd

starts with black point

- problems in the past

STYLE
ornate

- ostentatious
- vulgar

complicated

- calculating

LOWER CASE c

END STROKE
extended to right

- self-admiring

angular

- quick-minded

SHAPE
regular

- gracious
- idealistic
- simple

concave crescent

- constructive-minded
- frank

round

- gentle

square

- mechanical-minded

narrow

- idealistic
- shy

sharp at bottom

- resentful
- needs to get own way

sharp at top

- alert
- curious

covers letter

- shields self

almost circular

- shields self

starts below the line

- determined to succeed

**STARTING STROKE
reaching**

- enterprising

**STYLE
filled in**

- sensual

starts with a black point

- preoccupied with the past

enrolled

- calculating
- shrewd

like lower case e

- egotistic

CAPITAL D

END STROKE
extended to left (on
broad letter)

- concerned
  with the past
- irresponsible

"deletes" letter

- a dreamer

looped

- concerned
  with the past
- irresponsible

SHAPE
regular

- intelligent
- forthright

claw

- greedy

angular

- clever
- constructive-
  minded
- realistic
- rigid

narrow

- inhibited
- reserved
- shy

open at top

- talkative

open at bottom

- likes to gossip

tied at top

- reserved

unusual shape

- tendency to perversion

STARTING STROKE
reaching

- enterprising

STYLE
ornate

- ostentatious
- vulgar

looped

- flirtatious

looped at top and bottom

• vulgar

separated

• individualistic

SHAPE
regular

• self-confident

regular with tall stem

• idealistic
• spiritual
• has integrity

tall and narrow

• idealistic
• possibly religious

curved to right

• pleasure-loving

short stem

• humble
• independent
• proud

sharp

• resentful
• willful

open at top

- talkative

open at bottom

- dishonest
- hypocritical
- unreliable

STARTING STROKE
left flag

- creative
- musical
- protective

loops over to right

- defensive

STYLE
scrolled

- family-orientated
- secretive

like a music note

- musical

Greek

- aesthetic
- flirtatious
- poetic

looped

- sensitive
- vain

filled with ink

● sensual

knotted

● diplomatic

retraced

● dignified
● hypo-
chondriac

CAPITAL E

END STROKE
underlines word

E

● vain

SHAPE
regular

E

● cultured
● literate
● direct

narrow

E

● inhibited
● reserved
● shy

rounded

● warm

angular

- clever
- realistic
- quick

double concave arcs

- cultured
- a good observer
- quick-minded

unusual shape

- tendency to perversion

extended middle stroke

- cautious

STARTING STROKE
long

- ambitious
- quarrelsome

cuts through from left

- appearances are important

arcs to left

- avarice

joins with loop at top

- has difficulty mastering own affairs

enrolled

- sensitive

**STYLE
enrolled**

- egotistic
- greedy

ornate

- ostentatious
- vulgar

overstroked

- neurotic

LOWER CASE e

**END STROKE
short (on regular letter)**

- reticent

long (on regular letter)

- generous

overextended loop

- selfish

extends to upper right

- a dreamer

slopes down

- dominant
- egotistic

long, slopes down

- intolerant

extends to left

- cautious

loops to left

- tenacious

curled

- stubborn

SHAPE
regular

- friendly

STYLE
no loop

- critical
- quick-thinking

narrow loop

- critical
- narrow-minded

broad loop

- broadminded
- casual
- direct
- friendly
- outspoken

filled with ink

- sensual

Greek

- aesthetic
- cultured

CAPITAL F

SHAPE
regular

F

- intelligent
- literary
- direct

narrow

- inhibited
- reserved
- shy

angular triangular loop

- emotionally disappointed

rounded at top

- a dreamer

**STYLE
top stroke covers word**

- patronizing
- protective

crosslike

- fatalistic

knotted in middle

- cautious

flowing

- artistic
- sensitive

wavy

- has a sense of fun

ornate

- ostentatious
- vulgar

LOWER CASE f

SHAPE
regular

- artistic
- intelligent
- straight-forward

narrow

- emotionally repressed
- inhibited

STYLE
block lettered

- cultured

crosslike

- fatalistic

sharp loops at bottom

- resentful
- uncom-promising

triangular lower loop to left

- emotionally or sexually inhibited
- dislikes interference

triangular lower loop to right

- sexually disappointed

simplified strokes

- resentful
- uncom-promising

plain, top and bottom balanced

- intelligent
- artistic
- well-organized

balanced at top and bottom double loop

- well-organized
- managerial ability

fluid, with double loop

- original
- well-organized
- fluid thinker

no upper loop

- unable to apply objectivity to problem solving

long upper loop

- has ideas that need grounding in reality

full upper loop

- articulate
- needs grounding in reality

no lower loop; full upper loop

- poor organization
- needs grounding in reality

narrow upper loop

- narrow-minded

no lower loop

- lacks practical foundation

full lower loop

- a creative doer

full lower loop; no upper loop

- creative
- impractical

large lower loop

- creative

bulging lower loop

- food-oriented

enlarged lower loop

- active
- energetic
- poor organizer

open lower loop

- austere
- unconcerned with image

open lower loop; no upper loop

- forms own opinions

knotted

- tough
- thorough

knotted with a large loop

- pride in own and family's achievements

figure eight lower loop

- sometimes reveals female homosexuality

CAPITAL G

END STROKE arcs to left

- irresponsible in sexual or financial matters

SHAPE regular

- intelligent
- literary
- straight-forward

narrow

- inhibited
- reserved
- shy

concave arc

- constructive minded

unusual shape

- tendency to perversion

STARTING STROKE
arcs to left

- avarice

STYLE
large top loop

- a dreamer

large bottom loop

- egotistic

triangular lower loop

- sexually disappointed

Greek

- aesthetic
- cultured
- literary talent

ornate

- ostentatious
- vulgar

LOWER CASE g

AS CAPITAL G

- modest

END STROKE
swings upward

- imaginative
- optimistic about sex and money

swings out and up

- altruistic

trails to left

- contemplative
- poetic attitude to sensuality

swings down

- despondent about sex or money
- vain

SHAPE
regular

- demonstrative
- imaginative
- warm

STYLE
straight downstroke

- determined
- down-to-earth
- independent
- fatalistic
- physically active

long, looped downstroke

- materialistic
- restless
- restrictive attitude to sex

short downstroke

- sexually anxious/ restless
- lacks physical strength
- timid

crossed downstroke

- fears loss or rejection
- disappointed in past sexual relationship

down stroke arcs to right

- constructive
- makes visions a reality

like the number 9

- has a sense for figures

no lower loop; two strokes

- austere

lower loop arcs to left

- sexually irresponsible

terminal check to right

- sexually frustrated
- mildly aggressive

terminal check to left

- sexually frustrated
- impatient
- timid

triangular lower loop pointing to left; horizontally closed

- emotionally or sexually disappointed
- resentful
- tyrannical

triangular lower loop with horizontal base

- needs a material basis

enrolled to right

- egotistic
- greedy

lower loop open to left

- erotic elusiveness

slanted to right; terminal check to left

- expresses sexuality with negative emotions

slanting to right; regular shape

- emotionally tied to a nurturing figure

wide, open lower loop

- inflated sexual imagination
- gregarious
- loyal
- strong libido

inflated lower loop

- inflated sexual imagination
- materialistic

broad lower loop arcs to left

- artistic tendencies
- needs security
- sensual

broad, short, closed lower loop

- abnormal attachment to mother or past

small lower loop, open

- sexually inhibited

small lower loop, closed

- clannish
- selects friends carefully

loop crosses below baseline

- frustrated sexually or financially

enrolled

- greedy

curled lower loop

- sexually insincere
- impotent

circular lower loop (closed)

- sexual problems (in males) such as impotence

head wide open

● talkative

knotted

● a twisted attitude to sex or money matters

shaky

● sexually anxious
● weak sex drive

double lower loop

● vain

broken line

● sexually anxious
● weak sex drive
● a poor saver

lower loop in figure eight

● may indicate female homosexuality

CAPITAL H

END STROKE extended to right

● self-admiring

SHAPE regular

● intelligent
● straight-forward
● a reader

broad

- extravagant

STYLE
involved crossbar

- able to get out
  of situations

narrow

- inhibited
- reserved
- shy

enriched

- able to get out
  of situations

tall and narrow

- inhibited

ornate

- ostentatious
- vulgar

LOWER CASE h

END STROKE
extends down to left

- uncom-
  promising

SHAPE
regular

- cultured

tall and narrow

- idealistic
- opinionated
- proud

STARTING STROKE
tall

- idealistic
- opinionated
- proud

tall with hook

- a dreamer

short

- a disbeliever in spiritual values

short with small loop

- realistic
- unimaginative
- lacking in spiritual values

long and curled

- emotional
- sensitive

straight at acute angle

- hypo-chondriac
- opinionated
- rigid
- self-torturing

STYLE
retraced

- resentful

enrolled

- egotistic

ornate

- inflated sexual imagination

CAPITAL I

**END STROKE
arcs to left**

- avoids responsibility

arcs up and out to left

- contemplative

**SHAPE
regular**

- businesslike
- cultured
- intelligent
- direct

large

- megalo-maniac

narrow

- inhibited
- reserved
- shy

small

- inferiority complex

square

- aggressive

convex arc

- egotistic
- intelligent

large, convex arc

- megalomaniac

slight convex arc

- takes easy way out

STYLE
upper bar longer than lower bar

- mother influence

lower bar longer than upper bar

- father influence

slants to right

- puts self first

spaced

- erratic
- feels guilty about the past

dot on top

- idiosyncratic

single straight line

- clear
- concise
- mature
- modest

one stroke that slants to left

- guilt complex

curls to left

- doesn't like people

curls to left at top; bottom extends to left

- chatty
- has sense of humor

looped to left at bottom

- egotistic
- greedy

enrolled at bottom

- egotistic
- greedy

like the number 1

- relates to numbers

like the number 9

- relates to numbers

like the number 7

- relates to numbers

looped at top

- fixed ideas
- shrewd

circle at top

- humorous
- uncomplicated

circular

- defensive

like a dollar sign

- money-oriented

thin upper loop

- a keen mind
- resents mother

large upper loop

- likes to talk about self

tall upper loop

- imaginative
- believes him or herself to be different

one loop with end stroke extending to left

- father figure missing from writer's life

upper loop crossed out

- rejects self

double loop (wide)

- energetic
- powerful
- concerned with physical and material world

double loop (narrow)

- forceful
- rejects father

reduced upper loop

- repressed
- timid

LOWER CASE i

AS CAPITAL LETTER

- undervalues self

**SHAPE
regular**

- careful
- cautious
- pedantic
- precise

STYLE
regular with heavy dot

- materialistic
- strong-willed
- perhaps depressed

regular with light dot

- lacking energy
- sensitive
- timid

regular with circular dot

- egotistic
- eccentric
- inability to face facts

regular with high dot

- creative
- curious
- imaginative
- orderly

regular with low dot

- aggressive
- assertive
- exacting

regular with concave dot

- observant

regular with convex dot

- neurotic

regular with dot like a comma

- sarcastic
- witty

**regular with dot
like a dash (going up)**

- aggressive
- clever
- enthusiastic
- impatient
- witty

**regular with dot like a
dash (going down)**

- opinionated
- tempera-
  mental

dot to right

- curious
- enthusiastic
- impulsive

dot to left

- cautious
- procrastinates

dot clublike

- brutal
- sensual

no dot

|

- careless

triangular "dot"

- aggressive
- critical
- humorous
- quick-witted

arced "dot"

- deceitful
- diplomatic

crescent-shaped dot

- critical
- discriminating

concave crescent

- humorous
- sarcastic
- vivacious

connected to next letter

- ability for scientific work

CAPITAL J

END STROKE
broad loop

- inflated sexual imagination
- loyal
- strong libido

closed loop

- inflated sexual imagination
- gregarious
- loyal
- strong libido

closed, large loop

- inflated sexual imagination
- gregarious
- loyal
- strong libido

broad, curved loop

- artistic tendencies
- needs security
- sensual

low, wide loop

- abnormal attachment to mother or past

midway loop

- frustrated sexually or financially

hooked

- sexually inhibited

"deletes" letter

- imaginative
- optimistic about sex and money

trails to left

- contemplative
- poetic attitude to sexuality

reaching up to right, midway loop

- altruistic

small circle

- clannish
- tends to select friends carefully

arcs down to right

- despondent about sex or money
- vain

curled

- sexually insincere
- impotent

enrolled

- greedy

arcs to right

- sexually irresponsible

check mark

- sexually frustrated
- mildly aggressive
- impatient
- timid

triangular

- emotionally or sexually disappointed
- resentful
- tyrannical

SHAPE
regular

- demonstrative
- imaginative
- warm

STYLE
hook missing

- determined
- down-to-earth
- independent
- fatalistic
- physically active

long, looped
downstroke

- materialistic
- restless
- restricted attitude to sex

short downstroke

- sexually anxious or restless
- lacks physical strength
- timid

reversed downstroke

- constructive
- makes visions a reality

broken

- sexually anxious
- weak sex drive

regular with loop joined to base

- sexual abnormality (in males)
- impotence

shaky

- sexually anxious
- weak sex drive

backward-slanting

- erotic elusiveness

forward-slanting, angular

- expresses sexuality with negative emotions

forward-slanting, curved

- emotionally tied to a nurturing figure

LOWER CASE j

**END STROKE
open to left**

● immature

loop to left

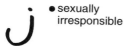

● sexually
irresponsible

**horizontally
sweeping to left**

● typical of male
homosexual

claw

● money-
minded

triangular (open)

● impress-
ionable

check mark

● aggressive

triangular (closed)

● aggressive

**STYLE
enrolled**

● greedy

looped

- egotistic

forms figure eight

- associated with female homosexuality

broad, large loop

- imaginative

CAPITAL K

SHAPE
regular

- intelligent
- literary
- mechanical

long upper stroke

- enterprising

short lower stroke

- ambitious

STYLE
long lower stroke

- defensive
- self-admiring
- uncompromising

disjointed lower stroke

- many ideas
- poor organizer

curved, disjointed second stroke

- afraid of the opposite sex
- cool
- distant

like the letter x

- antagonistic
- greedy for money

point though bar

- resents the opposite sex

knotted

- capable
- thorough
- tough
- likes people and sex

large knot

- thinking of past erotic experiences

enrolled

- egotistic

curled back at top

- eccentric

LOWER CASE k

SHAPE
regular

 • literary

STYLE
long lower stroke

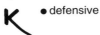 • defensive

long, lower stroke
and closed at top

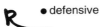 • defensive

lower stroke
extended to far right

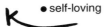 • self-loving

lower stroke extends to
far right and top closed

 • self-loving

tall first stroke

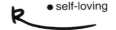 • enterprising

tall first stroke and
top closed

 • enterprising

inflated initial loop

• creative
• emotional
• imaginative

tall, narrow initial loop

- opinionated
- religious

closed, rounded head

- rebellious

knotted

- proud
- thorough

double knot

- concerned with image

double loop

- unconcerned with image

CAPITAL L

END STROKE underlining word

- self-admiring

SHAPE regular

- cultured
- literary

STARTING STROKE
check mark

- argumentative
- greedy for money

STYLE
ornate

- egotistic
- greedy
- insincere
- vulgar

enrolled

- faddy
- shrewd

initial loop

- sensitive

crossed by two bars

- money-motivated

heavy lower bar

- subject to mood changes

large loop to left

- vain

small loop to left

- materialistic
- positive
- reserved
- vain

large initial loop

● generous

LOWER CASE l

END STROKE
hook to right

● good
  judgment

check mark to right

● obstinate

SHAPE
straight line

● intuitive
● sensible
● quick-minded

narrow

● opinionated
● philosophical
● reserved

broad

● broadminded
● generous
● imaginative
● philosophical

tall

● likes to
  organize
  and make
  speeches
● a visionary

STARTING STROKE
long

- ambitious
- industrious
- quarrelsome

STYLE
sharp

- critical
- curious
- has high aspirations

sharp at top and bottom

- needs to get own way
- resentful

amended or overwritten

- hypo-chondriac

like a zero

- relates to figures

CAPITAL M

END STROKE
trails to left

- defensive

circular

- egotistic
- greedy

AN A-Z OF LETTER FORMS

SHAPE
regular

- cultured

wide

- extravagant

rounded

- extravagant

narrow, pointed

- inhibited
- mean

narrow, rounded

- inhibited
- mean

tall and narrow, pointed

- idealistic
- religious
- shrewd

tall and narrow, rounded

- idealistic
- religious
- shrewd

STARTING STROKE
large loop to left

- professionally jealous
- likes to handle money
- sense of humor

small loop to left

- personally jealous

arc starting beneath letter

- actor
- orator
- poser

dot to left

- enjoys material achievements

large dot to far left

- concerned with the past

large, low hook

- egotistic
- greedy

small hook

- good-natured
- sense of humor

sharp hook

- has a dry sense of humor

high, fat circle

- proud
- secretive
- sensitive

curly

- desires responsibility but is unable to handle it

tiny circle

- jealous

pointed left hook

- underhanded

check mark

- a gambler
- quick-tempered

STYLE
curved

- tactful

small center stem, pointed

- tactless

small center stem, rounded

- tactless

tall starting stroke rounded top

- egotistic

tall starting stroke; pointed at top

- egotistic

tall second stroke; pointed at top

- ambitious
- envious
- immature

tall second stroke; rounded at top

- ambitious
- envious
- immature
- seeking approval

lower second stroke; pointed top

- condescending
- diplomatic
- dislikes compromise
- proud

lower second stroke; rounded top

- condescending
- dislikes compromise
- proud

square

- technically skilled

pointed

- critical
- impatient
- probing

block

- aesthetic

curly

● conventional

ornate

● ostentatious
● vulgar

looped

● vain

overwritten

● tense

three arches

● idiosyncratic

LOWER CASE m

**END STROKE
high**

● likes to be
  well thought of

doesn't reach baseline

● lacks mental
  discipline
● dishonest

reaches below baseline

- has a temper

narrow

- timid

"deletes" letter

- suicidal tendencies

STARTING STROKE
small circle

- jealous

curly

- repressed
- shrewd

small check mark

- fussy

SHAPE
wide and round

- imaginative
- insincere

reaching

- egotistic
- proud

high loop

- worries

broad sweep

- acquisitive
- possessive

STYLE
three arches

- under mental strain

rounded

- creative
- gentle
- logical
- works with hands

peaked

- critical
- works with mind

triple upper loops

- clairvoyant

threadlike

- manipulative
- worries about others

like the letter w

- superficial thinker

very rounded

- childlike

oddly shaped

- sexual quirkiness

high loops

- musical

enrolled

- egotistic
- secretive

short middle stroke

- ambitious

"sacred heart"

- aristocratic
- pretentious

long middle stroke

- dependent on public opinion

high initial peak

- dependent on private opinion

unformed

- versatile
- hysterical
- indecisive

CAPITAL N

END STROKE
extends to right

- patronizing

reaches up

- enterprising

SHAPE
regular

- cultured

wide

- extravagant

wide and curved

- extravagant

narrow

- inhibited
- mean

narrow, curved

- inhibited
- mean

tall and narrow

- idealistic
- religious
- shrewd

tall and narrow; curved

- idealistic
- religious
- shrewd

arch

- tactful

square

- technically skilled

**STARTING STROKE
dot to left**

- enjoys material achievements

large dot extends to left

- concerned with the past

broad and sweeping

- egotistic
- greedy

at top of letter

- good-natured
- sense of humor

hooked

- dry humor

curled

- desires responsibility but is unable to handle it

STYLE
ornate

- ostentatious
- vulgar

overwritten

- tense

block

- aesthetic

small loop

- personally jealous

large loop

- professionally jealous

excessive loop

- likes to handle money
- sense of humor

END STROKE
wavy

- versatile

"deletes" letter

- suicidal tendencies

doesn't reach baseline

- ambitious
- dishonest

trails to left

- dislikes compromise

below baseline

- has a temper

curly

- repressed
- shrewd

SHAPE
broad

- wasteful

narrow

- inhibited

square

- mechanical-minded

rounded

- creative
- gentle
- works with hands

angular

- analytical-minded

STARTING STROKE
circular

- jealous

check mark

- fussy

high

- egotistic
- proud

small loop

 • worries

broad and sweeping

 • acquisitive
• possessive

STYLE
peaked

 • critical
• works with mind

looped

 • clairvoyant

enrolled

 • egotistic
• secretive

"sacred heart"

 • aristocratic
• pretentious

unformed

 • versatile
• hysterical
• indecisive

CAPITAL O

SHAPE
regular

- intelligent
- straightforward
- unpretentious

narrow

- inhibited
- reserved
- shy

wide

- show-off

STYLE
like a zero

- relates to figures

open at top

- frank
- friendly
- honest
- sincere
- talkative

open at bottom

- hypocritical

overwritten

- neurotic

with hook

- deceitful

knotted

 ● secretive

large loop

 ● sense of humor

looped

 ● quick-thinking

odd shape

 ● sexually perverse

END STROKE
enrolled

● cunning
● dishonest
● evasive
● selfish

check mark

● greedy
● perhaps resentful

enrolled, with hook

● deceiver

SHAPE
regular

● honest
● reserved
● perhaps secretive

large and full

- emotional
- generous

filled in

- sensual

narrow

- secretive

like a lower case e

- clever

STYLE
like a zero

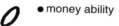

- money ability

open at top

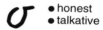

- honest
- talkative

sharp at bottom

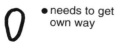

- needs to get own way

open to left

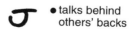

- talks behind others' backs

open at bottom

- dishonest
- lacks moral values

narrow knot

- tells white lies

tied on right

- discreet
- may not be honest with others

open with double loop

- talkative
- not always truthful

tied on left

- may not be honest with self
- rational

dangling hook

- preoccupied with sex

double knot

- dishonest with self and others

CAPITAL P

END STROKE
crosses first stroke

- discreet
- reserved

hooked to left

- money-minded

enrolled claw

- vulgar

SHAPE
regular

- cultured
- intelligent

tall

- proud
- vain

narrow

- inhibited
- reserved
- shy

STYLE
inflated

- egotistic
- imaginative

disjointed

- constructive-minded

looped over word

- generous
- protective

embellished

- vulgar

distorted

- sexually abnormal

slightly enrolled

- business-minded
- enterprising

enrolled

- shrewd
- has fixed ideas

dot in loop

- enjoys material success

separated up- and downstrokes

- austere
- talkative

LOWER CASE p

SHAPE
regular

- cultured

STARTING STROKE
high

- argumentative
- charitable
- enterprising

high check mark

- argumentative
- charitable
- enterprising

short

- expects pay for favors

large and looped

- argumentative
- imaginative

small and looped

- quarrelsome

STYLE
two disjointed arcs, pointing right

- creative

two disjointed arcs, pointing left

- constructive-minded

like the number 9

- interested in figures

open top

- talkative

open at bottom

- talks to animals and self

long lower loop

- likes physical activity
- hypochondriac

large loop

- likes physical activity
- hypochondriac

retraced lower loop

- likes physical activity
- hypochondriac

"rocker" P

- argumentative
- feels resentful about past

CAPITAL Q

SHAPE
regular

● clear thinker

thick second stroke

● brutal
● vigorous

STYLE
reversed

● idiosyncratic

LOWER CASE q

END STROKE
hook to left

● money-minded

looped to right

● altruistic

inflated hook

● inflated sexual imagination

enrolled

● greedy

SHAPE
regular

- demonstrative
- imaginative
- warm

STYLE
short stem

- sexually restless
- timid
- lacking physical strength

curved stem

- constructive
- makes visions a reality

heavy stem

- energetic

like a music note

- musical

tied on right

- may not be truthful to others

slanted to right

- emotionally tied to mother figure

open top

- talkative

wobbly

- weak sex drive
- sexually anxious

CAPITAL R

END STROKE
long

- obstinate

short

- ambitious

SHAPE
regular

- cultured
- intelligent

tall and narrow

- inhibited
- proud
- reserved
- shy

square

- practical

angular

- clever
- realistic
- resentful
- rigid

STARTING STROKE
loop to left

- egotistic

reaches up

- enterprising

STYLE
large upper loop

- friendly
- kind

ornate

- ostentatious
- vulgar

END STROKE
drooping

- a quick thinker

check mark

- changeable

enrolled

- a daydreamer

reaches over
top of letter

- distorts facts
- self-protective

SHAPE
regular

- cultured
- able to express thoughts in writing

narrow

- inhibited

arch

- dull
- lazy
- unobservant

STARTING STROKE
high

- critical
- curious

STYLE
looped

- prejudiced
- vain
- sings to self and others

"tabletop"

- broadminded about religion
- works with hands

peaked

- observant
- a sharp mind

knot on first stroke

- sings to self

knot on last stroke

 ● sings to others

CAPITAL S

END STROKE
hook to left

 ● deceitful

long, trailing

 ● enterprising

curved back to left

 ● irresponsible

SHAPE
regular

 ● cultured
● intelligent

broad, sweeping

 ● greedy
● vulgar

narrow

 ● inhibited
● reserved
● shy

AN A-Z OF LETTER FORMS

tall

- imaginative

ornate

- ostentatious
- vulgar

angular

- aggressive
- persistent
- rigid

like lower case s

- modest

STARTING STROKE
long

- difficult
- a hard worker

crossed by one
vertical bar

- relates to
  money

STYLE
reversed

- idiosyncratic

like dollar sign

- money-
  minded

curved back on itself

● irresponsible

like a treble clef

● musical

LOWER CASE s

**END STROKE
enrolled**

● fussy
● greedy
● shrewd

looped

● tenacious

horizontal

● hidden greed

**SHAPE
tall**

● repressed

curly

● greedy
● egotistic

rounded

● artistic
● kind

angular

- persistent
- rigid

STARTING STROKE
"deletes" letter

- imaginative

STYLE
printed

- a reader

curly

- greedy

sharp top

- critical
- curious
- stubborn

sharp top and closed

- critical
- curious
- stubborn

rounded top

- yielding

closed

- secretive
- shrewd

CAPITAL T

END STROKE
extends over word

- patronizing
- protective

loop to left

- proud

SHAPE
regular

- intelligent

tall and narrow

- inhibited
- reserved
- shy

STYLE
flowing

- fussy
- vulgar

ornate

- ostentatious
- vulgar

LOWER CASE t

CROSSBAR
light

- non-competitive
- sensitive

tapering

- indecisive
- quick to give up

heavy

- firm
- strong-willed
- quick to anger

gets heavier

- brutal
- slow-tempered
- vigorous

gets sharper

- malicious critic
- hasty temper

high

- a daydreamer

at top of letter

- ambitious
- bossy
- capable
- idealistic
- proud

midway position

- organized
- precise
- self-controlled

low

- depressed
- humble
- obedient
- patient
- subordinate

long

- enthusiastic
- imaginative
- protective

long and sharp

- cruel
- sarcastic

short

- lacks control
- underachieves

crosses two letter t's

- plans actions and efforts

taste

absent

- absent-minded
- physical weakness
- inattentive to detail

up-sloping

- aggressive
- ambitious
- curious
- egotistic
- optimistic

heavy and up-sloping

- aggressive
- optimistic

down-sloping and tapered

- bossy
- domineering

down-sloping

- critical
- determined
- domineering
- resentful
- sulky

down-sloping and getting thicker

- aggressive
- brutal
- destructive
- determined

wavy and down-sloping

- obstinate

double

- dual-natured

like a cross

- religious-leaning

CROSSBAR regular

- consistent
- positive

curved

- wants to control others
- weak health

curved up

- easygoing
- over-compliant
- self-controlled
- sense of humor

undulating

- frivolous
- fun-loving
- humorous

disjointed and up-sloping; on left

- ambitious
- demanding
- seeks recognition

joined on right at top

- ambitious
- a leader
- intelligent

detached; on right

- accepts a challenge
- impulsive

right hook

- greedy

small, on right

- lacks confidence

longer to right

- easily irritated
- enthusiastic
- impulsive
- tactless

AN A-Z OF LETTER FORMS

tapers to top right

- a dreamer
- idealistic

END STROKE "deletes" letter

- egotistic
- jealous
- self-pitying

dash to right

- tenacious

curves back

- egotistic

short dash on left

- hesitant to use leadership abilities

midpoint bar to left

- cautious
- moderate

low on left, horizontal

- cautious
- inferior
- procrastinator

curves to left

- attempts to control procrastination

hooked to right

- acquisitive
- possessive

hook on left and right

- persistent
- sulky

check mark

- determined
- easygoing

STYLE
small stem

- independent worker
- low ambition
- timid

tall stem

- idealistic

open stem

- indolent
- slow

tall stem with strong bar

- ambitious
- strong character

retraced stem

- repressed
- inexpressive

looped stem

- articulate
- sensitive
- talkative

hooked on top

- vain

like a lower case r

- easygoing
- uses initiative

starlike

- coercive
- has a sense of responsibility

tied star

- persistent
- resentful
- sense of responsibility

star with long end stroke

- quick-tempered
- untamable

knotted

- tough
- thorough

large loop

- demonstrative
- opinionated
- proud of own achievements
- stubborn

triangular

- disappointed
- sensitive

CAPITAL U

SHAPE
regular

- intelligent
- unpretentious

STARTING STROKE
curved

- sense of humor

narrow

- inhibited
- reserved
- shy

looped

- sense of humor

angular

- persistent
- resistant

sweep from
below the baseline

- actor
- poser

STYLE
unduating

• versatile

ornate

• ostentatious
• vulgar

LOWER CASE u

SHAPE
angular

• resistant

STARTING STROKE
regular

• pull from
  the past

broad

• odd
  imagination

arched

• fearful
• protective
• appearances
  important

regular

• good listener
• kind
• needs to be
  accepted

STYLE
retraced

• repressed
• unexpressive

wavy line

● versatile

CAPITAL V

END STROKE
reaching up

● enterprising
● rebellious

"deletes" letter

● disappointed

extends over word

● altruistic
● protective

SHAPE
regular

● clear-minded
● intelligent

hooked

● disappointed

narrow

● inhibited
● reserved
● shy

curved

● unaggressive

STYLE
enriched and
horizontally crossed

● fussy
● vulgar

STARTING STROKE
extended

● sense of humor

ornate

● ostentatious
● vulgar

LOWER CASE v

END STROKE
extends up

● enterprising

SHAPE
regular

● intelligent

hooked

● vulgar

rounded

● kind
● unaggressive

CAPITAL W

END STROKE
round

- generous

extends up

- enterprising

curves back

- enterprising

SHAPE
regular

- cultured
- intelligent

narrow, angular

- inhibited
- reserved
- shy

narrow, curved

- inhibited
- reserved
- shy

STARTING STROKE
wavy

- sense of humor

figure eight

- sense of humor

sweeping

● vulgar

curled

● likes responsibility

STYLE
closed and round

● sexually eccentric

ornate

● ostentatious
● vulgar

LOWER CASE w

END STROKE
extends up

● enterprising

small loop

● poetic taste

SHAPE
regular

● clear-thinking

angular

● analytical

curved

- lives in past
- fearful of future

STARTING STROKE
regular

- resisting

CAPITAL X

SHAPE
regular

- intelligent
- precise
- with fighting spirit

narrow

- inhibited
- reserved
- shy

rounded

- talkative
- lacks precision
- difficulty adapting

STYLE
extended downstroke

- hot-tempered

extended upstroke

- ambitious
- enterprising

tapering upstroke

- hot-tempered
- concerned with past

separated stroke

- works toward future

ornate

- ostentatious
- vulgar

LOWER CASE x

SHAPE
regular

- intelligent
- precise
- with fighting spirit

STYLE
extended downstroke

- hot-tempered

narrow

- inhibited
- reserved
- shy

extended upstroke

- ambitious
- enterprising

rounded

- talkative
- lacks precision
- difficulty adapting

tapering upstroke

- hot-tempered
- concerned with past

separated stroke

 • works toward future

ornate

 • ostentatious
• vulgar

CAPITAL Y

END STROKE
extended to left

 • immature
• impressionable

hooked

 • avoids responsibility

horizontal

 • homosexual (male)

large loop

 • imaginative

check mark

 • avaricious

broad, open loop

 • greedy
• egotistic

SHAPE
regular

- intelligent

STYLE
vertical main stroke

- good judgment

LOWER CASE y

END STROKE
swings upward

- imaginative
- optimistic about sex and money

swings out and up

- altruistic

trails to left

- contemplative
- poetic attitude to sensuality

swings down

- despondent about sex and money
- vain

SHAPE
regular

- demonstrative
- imaginative
- warm

STYLE
straight downstroke

- determined
- down-to-earth
- independent
- fatalistic

long, looped downstroke

- materialistic
- restless
- restrictive attitude to sex

no lower loop; two strokes

- austere

short downstroke

- sexually anxious/restless
- lacks physical strength
- timid

lower loop arcs to left

- sexually irresponsible

crossed downstroke

- fears loss or rejection
- disappointed in past sexual relationship

terminal check to right

- sexually frustrated
- mildly aggressive

downstroke arcs to right

- constructive
- makes visions a reality

terminal check to left

- sexually frustrated
- impatient
- timid

triangular lower loop pointing to left; horizontally closed

- emotionally or sexually disappointed
- resentful
- tyrannical

triangular lower loop with horizontal base

- needs a material basis

enrolled to left

- egotistic
- greedy

lower loop open to left

- erotic elusiveness

slanted to right; terminal check to left

- suppressed sexuality with negative emotions

slanting to right; regular shape

- emotionally tied to a nurturing figure

wide, open lower loop

- inflated sexual imagination
- gregarious
- loyal
- strong libido

inflated lower loop

- inflated sexual imagination
- materialistic

broad lower loop arcs to left

- artistic tendencies
- needs security
- sensual

broad, short, closed lower loop

- abnormal attachment to mother or past

small lower loop, open

- sexually inhibited

small lower loop, closed

- clannish
- selects friends carefully

loop crosses below baseline

- frustrated sexually or financially

enrolled

- greedy

curled lower loop

- sexually insincere
- impotent

circular lower loop (closed)

- sexual problems (in males) such as impotence

shaky

- sexually anxious
- weak sex drive

broken line

- sexually anxious
- weak sex drive
- a poor saver

knotted

- a twisted attitude to sex or money matters

double lower loop

- vain

lower loop in figure eight

- may indicate female homosexuality

CAPITAL Z

END STROKE extends under word

- vain

reaches down

- critical
- depressed
- disappointed

curves down

- doesn't finish things

ornate

- ostentatious
- vulgar

SHAPE
regular

- cultured
- intelligent
- a reader

regular alternate

- cultured
- intelligent
- a reader
- easygoing

narrow

- inhibited
- reserved
- shy

narrow alternate

- inhibited
- reserved
- shy

LOWER CASE z

END STROKE
extends to right

● vain

extends down to right

● critical
● depressed
● disappointed

SHAPE
regular

● cultured
● intelligent

narrow

● inhibited
● reserved
● shy

CHARACTER TRAITS

Sometimes you may wish to identify whether a piece of
handwriting reveals certain character traits. For
example, if you are screening candidates for a job, it
may be useful to try to identify those individuals whose

Character traits listed:

aggressive	hypochondriac	rigid
ambitious	idealistic	sarcastic
artistic/creative	imaginative	secretive
constructive	impatient	sensitive
critical	independent	sensual
cultured	inhibited	shrewd
curious	intelligent	shy
defensive	irresponsible	straightforward
determined	jealous	talkative
diplomatic	literary	thorough
dishonest	loyal	timid
dreamy	materialistic	tough
egotistic	modest	uncompromising
enterprising	money-minded	vain
familiar with	neurotic	vulgar
figures	opinionated	well-organized
fatalistic	ostentatious	
fussy	protective	
generous	proud	
greedy	quarrelsome	
gregarious	quick-minded	
honest	realistic	
humble	resentful	
humorous	reserved	

character traits match your requirements. In this section you will find a list of some common character traits together with some examples of those letter forms which are believed to be representative of such traits. Always remember that any trait revealed by a letter form may be tempered by other aspects of the handwriting— all of which should be taken into account if you are to form a full and rounded analysis. You should also bear in mind that there are thousands of different letter forms, only some of which are provided here.

Each of the following boxes provides examples of letter forms which may indicate the trait listed in the top left corner of the box. Traits are listed in alphabetical order.

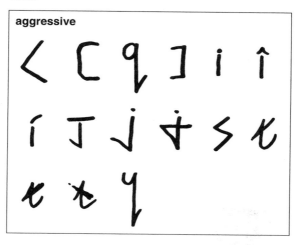

aggressive

ambitious

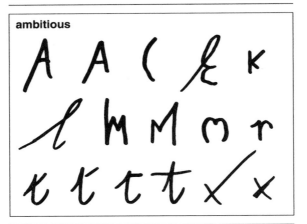

artistic/creative

constructive

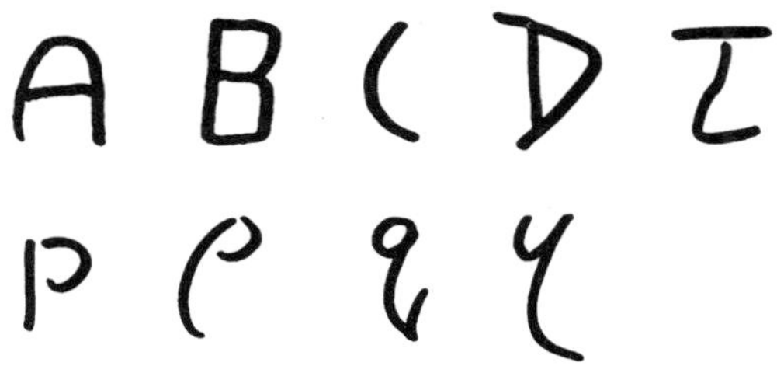

A B (D T

P P 9 4

critical

e e î í j

ϯ M m ϰ ß

ℓ t Z ⌐

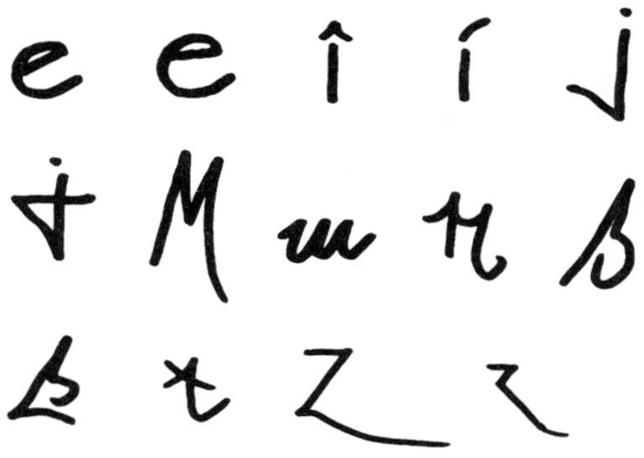

cultured

A E { F h

I L N P P

R W Z 3 z

curious

C i i l

n b l l

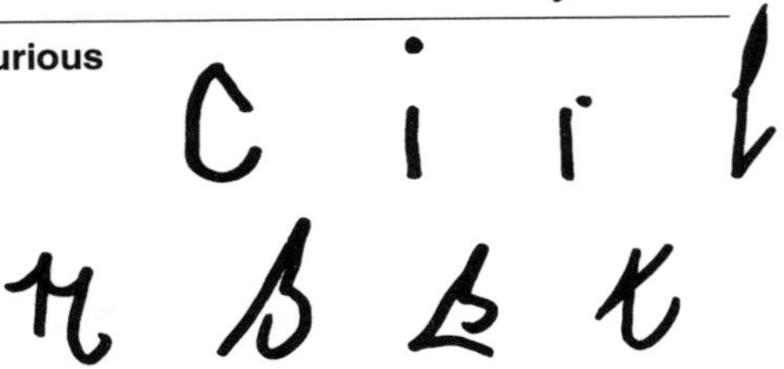

defensive

A & Q K R

determined

$B \quad 9 \quad T \quad t \quad t \quad 4$

diplomatic

$a \quad \hat{\imath} \quad M$

dishonest

$a \quad a \quad a \quad a \quad d$

a

dreamy

egotistic

enterprising

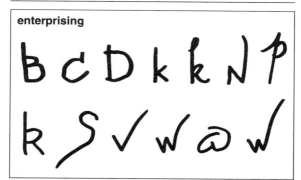

b c D k k N P
k S v w @ w

familiar with figures

13 6 9 1 1
9 0 0 P

fatalistic

t t 9 T 4

fussy

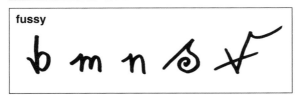

generous

A B e ʒ

greedy

u a b D E g

d d 1 L cm

cm O g g S t

gregarious

honest

A a a O

humble

b d t

humorous

b î m N Q σ
t u u N W

hypochondriac

idealistic

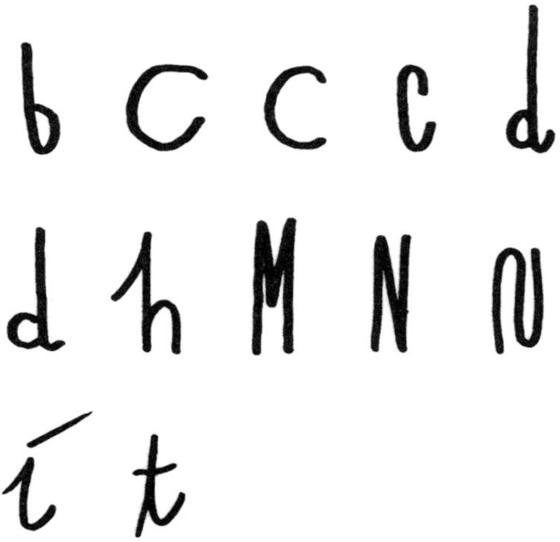

imaginative

impatient

independent

9 T Y

inhibited

A B C D E F G

M N O r S T U X

intelligent

A B C D F G

H K O R S T

U V W X Y Z

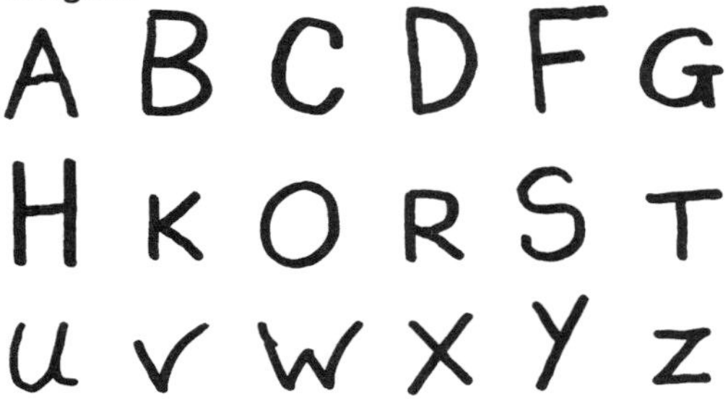

irresponsible

jealous

literary

loyal

materialistic

modest

money-minded

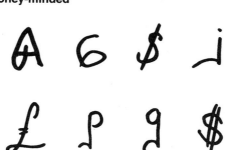

neurotic

opinionated

ostentatious

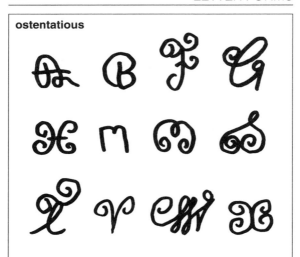

protective

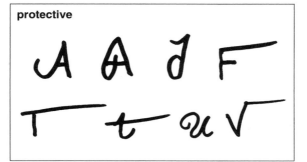

proud

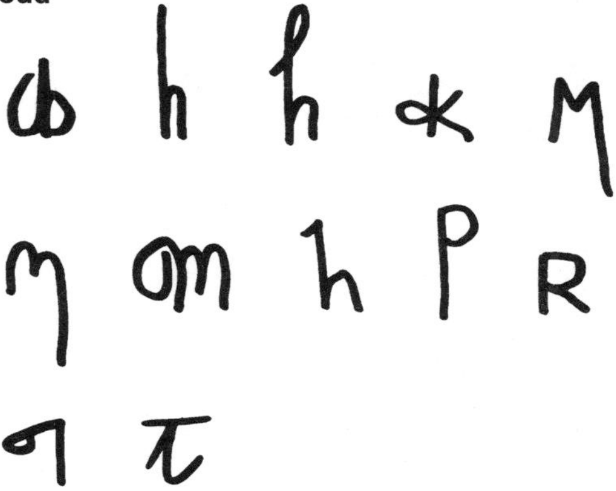

quarrelsome

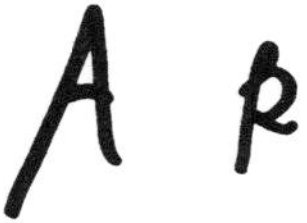

quick-minded

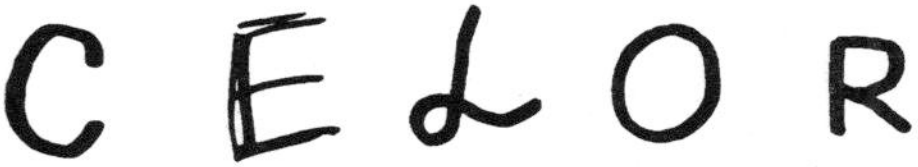

realistic

A B < D R

resentful

reserved

A B C D Ø

E F G H I

O P ℓ

rigid

A R S

sarcastic

secretive

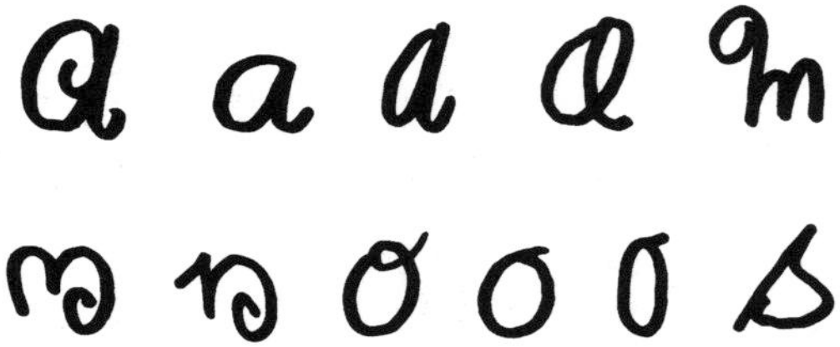

sensitive

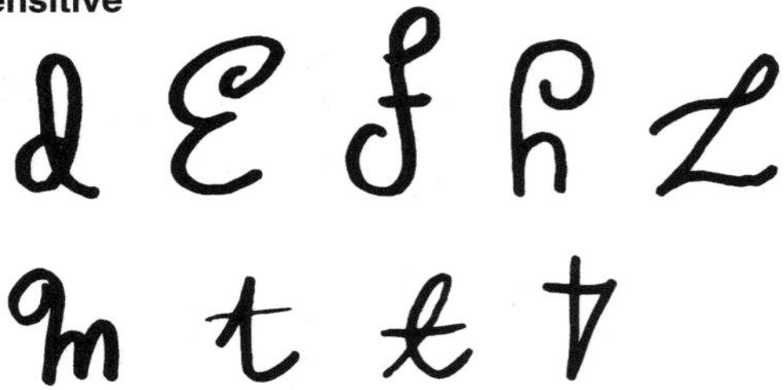

sensual

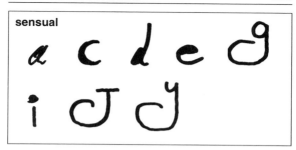

a c d e g

i J J y

shrewd

C G L M M

m N N s s

shy

A B C C D E F G

H I O W W X x

straightforward

f G H O

talkative

A a a B D

d g O o o

p p q

thorough

timid

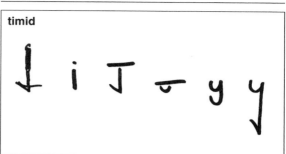

tough

uncompromising

vain

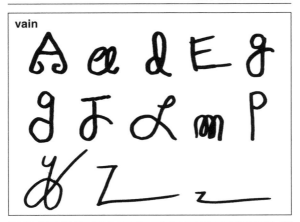

vulgar

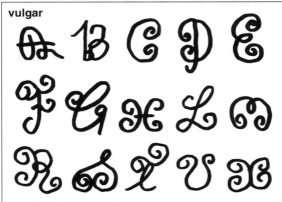

well-organized

INDEX

If you liked this book, you'll love this series:

Little Giant Book of Optical Illusions • Little Giant Book of "True" Ghost Stories • Little Giant Book of Whodunits • Little Giant Encyclopedia of Aromatherapy • Little Giant Encyclopedia of Baseball Quizzes • Little Giant Encyclopedia of Card & Magic Tricks • Little Giant Encyclopedia of Card Games • Little Giant Encyclopedia of Card Games Gift Set • Little Giant Encyclopedia of Dream Symbols • Little Giant Encyclopedia of Fortune Telling • Little Giant Encyclopedia of Gambling Games • Little Giant Encyclopedia of Games for One or Two • Little Giant Encyclopedia of Handwriting Analysis • Little Giant Encyclopedia of Magic • Little Giant Encyclopedia of Mazes • Little Giant Encyclopedia of Names • Little Giant Encyclopedia of Natural Healing • Little Giant Encyclopedia of One-Liners • Little Giant Encyclopedia of Palmistry • Little Giant Encyclopedia of Puzzles • Little Giant Encyclopedia of Spells & Magic • Little Giant Encyclopedia of Superstitions • Little Giant Encyclopedia of Toasts & Quotes • Little Giant Encyclopedia of Travel & Holiday Games • Little Giant Encyclopedia of Word Puzzles • Little Giant Encyclopedia of the Zodiac

Available at fine stores everywhere.